CULTURES OF THE WORLD
Uruguay

Cavendish
Square
New York

Published in 2019 by Cavendish Square Publishing, LLC
243 5th Avenue, Suite 136, New York, NY 10016
Copyright © 2019 by Cavendish Square Publishing, LLC

Third Edition

Cataloging-in-Publication Data

Names: Jermyn, Leslie. | Wong, Winnie. | Nevins, Debbie.
Title: Uruguay / Leslie Jermyn, Winnie Wong, and Debbie Nevins.
Description: New York : Cavendish Square, 2019. | Series: Cultures of the world | Includes glossary and index.
Identifiers: LCCN ISBN 9781502636447 (library bound) | ISBN 9781502636454 (ebook)
Subjects: LCSH: Uruguay--Juvenile literature.
Classification: LCC F2708.5 J47 2019 | DDC 989.5--dc23

Writers, Leslie Jermyn, Winnie Wong; Debbie Nevins, third edition
Editorial Director, third edition: David McNamara
Editor, third edition: Debbie Nevins
Designer, third edition: Jessica Nevins

Picture Researcher, third edition: Jessica Nevins

PICTURE CREDITS

Cover: Yaacov Dagan / Alamy Stock Photo
The photographs in this book are used with the permission of: p. 1 Iakov Filimonov/Shutterstock.com; p. 3, 6, 62, 64, 65, 111 DFLC Prints/Shutterstock.com; p. 5, 66 Ruslana Iurchenko/Shutterstock.com; p. 7, 10, 13, 51, 112 Ksenia Ragozina/Shutterstock.com; p. 8, 70, 86, 97 PABLO PORCIUNCULA/AFP/Getty Images; p. 12 Tupungato/Shutterstock.com; p. 14 Olaf Speier/Shutterstock.com; p. 15, 54 byvalet/Shutterstock.com; p. 16 (top) nwdph/Shutterstock.com; p. 16 (bottom) PKS Photography/Shutterstock.com; p. 17 (top) darock/Shutterstock.com; p. 17 (bottom) Tadas_Jucys/Shutterstock.com; p. 18 Joel Blit/Shutterstock.com; p. 19 Thomas Pereira Machado/Shutterstock.com; p. 20 R.M. Nunes/Shutterstock.com; p. 22 Prisma/UIG via Getty Images; p. 24 © North Wind Picture Archives; p. 25 Photo 12/Alamy Stock Photo; p. 27 Angela N Perryman/Shutterstock.com; p. 28 Janusz Pienkowski/Shutterstock.com; p. 29 Konstantinos Gavriilidis/Shutterstock.com; p. 30 Maximoangel/Shutterstock.com; p. 31 Juan Manuel Blanes/Wikimedia Commons/File:Juan Manuel Blanes - El Juramento de los Treinta y Tres Orientales.jpg; p. 32 DeAgostini/Getty Images; p. 33 rook76/Shutterstock.com; p. 36 Hoverfish/Wikimedia Commons/File:Museo de la Memoria.jpg/CC BY-SA 3.0; p. 37 Keystone Pictures USA/Alamy Stock Photo; p. 38 DANIEL CASELLI/AFP/Getty Images; p. 39 ALEJANDRO PAGNI/AFP/Getty Images; p. 40, 43, 46, 52, 77, 106 MIGUEL ROJO/AFP/Getty Images; p. 42 lvalin/Shutterstock.com; p. 44 Steve Allen/Shutterstock.com; p. 48 Pablo Bauza/Shutterstock.com; p. 56 ANGEL SARAVIA/AFP/Getty Images; p. 57 Michel Piccaya/Shutterstock.com; p. 60, 82 Don Mammoser/Shutterstock.com; p. 67 Paulo Fridman/Corbis via Getty Images; p. 68, 73, 92, 95, 114, 117, 119, 124, 127 Kobby Dagan/Shutterstock.com; p. 72, 80, 128 Matyas Rehak/Shutterstock.com; p. 75 Carlos Lebrato/Anadolu Agency/Getty Images; p. 83, 88, 94 lembi/Shutterstock.com; p. 91 Everett Historical/Shutterstock.com; p. 96 Neale Cousland/Shutterstock.com; p. 99 Andreea Dragomir/Shutterstock.com; p. 100 Janusz Pienkowski/Shutterstock.com; p. 101 Estampas de la Biblia by Juana de Ibarbourou/Wikimedia Commons/File:Juana de Ibarbourou from Estampas de la Biblia.jpg; p. 102 Carlos Alvarez/Getty Images; p. 104, 105 elbud/Shutterstock.com; p. 107 BoomerKC/File:Crash site.JPG/Wikimedia Commons; p. 108, 110 Ceswal/Shutterstock.com; p. 109 Rosalba Matta-Machado/Shutterstock.com; p. 113 Inspired By Maps/Shutterstock.com; p. 122 Karol Kozlowski/Shutterstock.com; p. 126 Iuliia Timofeeva/Shutterstock.com; p. 130 Hans Geel/Shutterstock.com; p. 131 Daniel Korzeniewski/Shutterstock.com; p. 137 Gil C/Shutterstock.com.

PRECEDING PAGE

The Palacio Salvo is a national historic monument in Montevideo, Uruguay.

Printed in the United States of America

CONTENTS

URUGUAY TODAY

URUGUAY IS A LATIN AMERICAN COUNTRY THAT IS SOMETIMES CALLED "the Switzerland of South America." But if that phrase conjures up images of snow-capped alpine peaks, the comparison couldn't be more wrong. Uruguay is relatively flat and the temperature rarely falls to freezing. Snow is virtually unknown there.

However, like Switzerland, Uruguay is a small country squeezed between giants—in its case, Argentina and Brazil. It's a peaceful, relatively affluent, democratic nation with a socially progressive government and a strong social safety net, which is paid for in fairly high taxes. And, like the Swiss, the Uruguayans are mostly—but not exclusively—white people of European descent.

The similarity extends only just so far, however, because Uruguay is really quite different in many ways. Unlike Switzerland, it is a coastal country, situated on the Atlantic Ocean and the Río de la Plata estuary. It lies well south of the equator—between the latitudes of 30 and 35 degrees south—and therefore its seasons are reversed compared to those in the Northern Hemisphere. The country has four

High-rise buildings overlook Pacitos Beach in Montevideo.

seasons, but they occur at the opposite ends of the calendar. When it's summer in North America, it's winter in Uruguay, though a generally mild one. The months of June, July, and August are cool and can be damp, dreary, and overcast. The months of December, January, and February are summertime, and a hot, humid summer at that.

That's when Uruguay's many beautiful beaches provide a welcome respite. Sandy, palm-lined beaches attract tourists from both inside and outside the country. In fact, Uruguay is a popular destination for expatriates from both Europe and the United States—especially folks who speak, or are willing to learn, Spanish. Like most of Latin America, aside from Brazil, Spanish is the primary language.

Uruguay's culture is decidedly South American—European inflected, but with a gaucho spirit. Like the cowboys of North America, the gauchos of South America are romanticized, historical heroes whose lifestyle of rugged

independence infuses the Uruguayan culture today. The gauchos herded cattle on the Pampas, or vast, low-lying grassy plains that stretch from Argentina to Brazil, covering virtually the entire country of Uruguay.

Cattle ranching is still a major enterprise in the country's rural interior. Gastronomically, meat is king—especially barbecued outdoors on huge grills. Woe be to the lonely vegetarian!

But then, Uruguay respects individuality and free choice, and has taken some very progressive turns in recent history. In 2006, under President Tabaré Vázquez's first term (2005—2010), smoking in public was outlawed. The president, after all, was an oncologist, or cancer doctor. In 2012, under President José Mujica (in office 2010—2015), Uruguay became the first country in South America to legalize abortion under limited circumstances. In 2013, it became only the second country in Latin America, after Argentina, to legalize same-sex marriage.

Modern-day gauchos ride side by side en route to a new cattle pasture in Minas.

A crowd of demonstrators rally for the legalization of cannabis outside the Legislative Palace in 2013.

That same year, it legalized the recreational use of cannabis, or marijuana—the first country in the world to do so. But then, Uruguay had never criminalized personal possession of drugs to begin with. The legal questions that the government needed to hammer out involved the production, regulation, and sale of the drug. In 2017, during Tabaré Vázquez's second term as president (since 2015), the law stipulated some tight controls. The marijuana industry was not to be a free-for-all. The government controls production, registers users, and authorizes pharmacies to sell it. Not wishing to see the country become an international destination for drug users, the law stipulates that only citizens and legal permanent residents are allowed to purchase or grow it.

Some of these actions may be understood in the context of Uruguay's deeply-entrenched separation of church and state, which, along with other reforms, dates to 1917. But its recent political transition to a left-leaning nation is no doubt partly due to its haunted past. The country fell under the control of an authoritarian, civic-military dictatorship from 1973 to 1985. It was a time of tremendous repression of human rights during which thousands of people were arrested for political reasons, and many subjected to torture and murder. After arrest, some people were simply never heard from again—people who came to be called the "disappeared."

Ghosts of a more distant past are still troubling the nation—the indigenous people, who were nearly eradicated by massacres in the nineteenth century; and the enslaved Africans who were forced to cross the Atlantic to serve white masters. Descendants of those Africans now make up about 4 to 12 percent of Uruguay's population, and remain among its poorest citizens.

Uruguay today is still coming to terms with those bad years and past sins. In his earlier life, the would-be president José Mujica joined the Tupamaros movement, an armed guerilla political group. After the military took over the government, he was imprisoned and spent thirteen captive years in squalid, isolated, and inhumane conditions which severely affected his health.

Those years in prison shaped his outlook on life. As president years later, Mujica became a champion for individual freedoms and became known as the "the world's humblest head of state." He led a very modest lifestyle and donated 90 percent of his presidential salary to charities. Both he and his successor, President Vázquez, are socialists, which marks a new direction for Uruguayan government. Meanwhile, the last of the brutal dictators, General Gregorio Álvarez, died in 2016, at age ninety-one, while serving a prison sentence for human rights abuses.

Where Uruguay goes from here remains to be seen. Perhaps the most hopeful portent of which way the wind will blow can be seen in the rows of wind mills crossing the Pampas. In less than a decade, Uruguay became a world leader in clean, renewable energy. In 2015, it produced 95 percent of its electricity from renewable sources, thereby sharply reducing its reliance on foreign oil. Buoyed by that success, the little country may take on some of its other problems—an aging population, polluted rivers, a slight rise in crime, a faltering education system—and surge confidently into the future.

GEOGRAPHY

A lighthouse stands on the shoreline in the small beach town of Jose Ignacio, Uruguay.

1

U RUGUAY IS A SMALL COUNTRY IN South America, sandwiched between the two largest countries of that continent—Brazil and Argentina. Located on the Atlantic seaboard, Uruguay covers an area of about 68,000 square miles (176,120 square kilometers), and is the second smallest sovereign nation in South America, after Suriname. The capital city, Montevideo, is the southernmost capital city in the Americas, and the third most southerly in the world, after Canberra, Australia, and Wellington, New Zealand.

The perimeter of Uruguay is 1,024 miles (1,648 km) long, including a coastline of 410 miles (660 km). To the south is the Río de la Plata ("Silver River") estuary where the Río Uruguay ("Uruguay River") empties into the Atlantic Ocean. The Río Uruguay separates Uruguay from Argentina on the west, and the Merín Lagoon marks the border with Brazil in the northeast. In the north, Uruguay and Brazil are separated by the Río Cuareim.

The most important river is the Río Negro, or Black River. It rises in the southern highlands of Brazil and flows west across the entire width of Uruguay to the Uruguay River. The river essentially divides the southern part of Uruguay from the north.

Uruguay is generally flatlands and rolling plains. It is watered by the Río de la Plata and the Río Uruguay. Most of the nation's agricultural activities take place around these rivers due to the rich alluvial soil found there. Uruguay enjoys a moderate, temperate climate. It is home to many different species of flora and fauna, but these are threatened by habitat loss.

This map of South America shows Uruguay's position on the continent.

The Río Negro is dammed in three locations by hydroelectric power stations. The Rincón del Bonete Reservoir, also called the Río Negro Reservoir—one of the largest artificial lakes in South America and the largest in Uruguay—was created in 1945 with the building of a dam near Paso de los Toros.

URUGUAY'S REGIONS

Uruguay is made up of gently rolling grass-covered plains with no hills over 1,686 feet (514 meters) above sea level—the highest point being Cerro Catedral ("Cathedral Hill"). It is located in the southeast of the country in the Cuchilla Grande mountain range.

The entirety of Uruguay lies within South America's Pampas region—a vast tract of fertile grassy lowlands or plains covering more than 290,000 square miles (750,000 sq. km). The Pampas also cover the southernmost part of Brazil, and eastern sections of Argentina.

Although there are no dramatic differences in geography across the country, there are four regions that differ noticeably in human settlement

patterns and land use. These regions are the countryside, or interior; the seacoast; the littoral, or river region; and the Greater Montevideo area.

A bucolic scene in the rural countryside of Uruguay.

THE INTERIOR This is the largest region, and it includes most of the central portion of the nation. It is mainly grassland with very little forest. Only 10.2 percent of the country is forested. These wooded areas, called gallery forests, grow along the edges of rivers. The soil of such an area is not very rich and therefore will not support intensive agriculture. Most of this land is used for raising cattle and sheep on large ranches.

THE ATLANTIC SEABOARD This is the band of land that stretches east from Montevideo in the south and then moves north toward Brazil along the Atlantic Ocean. Close to Montevideo the coastline is sandy and dotted with

Waves roll in on a sunny, summer day at La Pedrera beach.

vacation resorts and small settlements of people who commute to Montevideo to work. The shore turns north at Punta del Este, or "East Point"—the most popular vacation resort in Uruguay.

THE LITTORAL This is a narrow strip of fertile land on the shores of the Río de la Plata and the Río Uruguay to the west and north of Montevideo. The alluvial soil of the region, which is enriched by the periodic flooding of rivers, is the country's most arable land, and most of Uruguay's food crops are grown here. A bridge across the Uruguay River at Paysandú makes trade with Argentina very easy.

GREATER MONTEVIDEO Most of Uruguay's 3.47 million people live in this region—in Montevideo (population 1.7 million) and its neighboring departments of Canelones and San José. Metro Montevideo is the only large city in the county, and the rest of the urban population lives in some twenty to thirty small towns.

CLIMATE

Uruguay lies completely within the temperate zone, so the climate is moderate, with few extremes. There are four distinct seasons, but because Uruguay is south of the equator, the seasons are the reverse of those in North America. January is the middle of summer with temperatures ranging from 70 degrees Fahrenheit to 82°F (21 degrees Celsius to 28°C). July, the depth of winter, has average temperatures of 50°F to 61°F (10°C to 16°C).

Flowers bloom on a December day in Plaza Independencia in Montevideo.

There is no distinct rainy season, though there is slightly more rainfall in the winter. Since there are no mountains, rain falls fairly evenly across the country. Rainfall averages 36 inches (91 centimeters) yearly. Winter and spring are characterized by high winds that are subject to rapid shifts in direction. With no natural barriers to stop them, winds can be violent, and sometimes tornadoes develop. Occasionally, cold north winds from the plains of Argentina cause temperatures to plunge in the winter, while winds off the Atlantic Ocean in the summer bring cooler temperatures.

FLORA AND FAUNA

Uruguay has the smallest forested area of all the South American countries. Besides its gallery forests, tall prairie grass dominates the Uruguayan landscape. The gallery forests are a strip of wooded land that extends for 466 miles (750 km) along the Uruguay River. They contain a variety of trees, including hardwoods such as *algarrobo* (carob), *guayabo* (guava), *quebracho*, and *urunday*.

THE CAPYBARA *This South American mammal is the world's largest rodent—it can weigh up to 150 pounds (68 kilograms). It usually lives near water, and its eyes and ears are positioned very high on its head to allow it to swim easily. Its partially webbed feet also help with swimming. This animal is hunted extensively for its meat in many parts of South America today.*

In 2008, Andrés Rinderknecht and Ernesto Blanco, scientists from Montevideo, discovered a fossilized skull of the now extinct giant capybara (Josephoartigasia monesi) stored in Uruguay's National History and Anthropology Museum. The ancient rodents lived millions of years ago in South America and were positively gigantic compared to today's capybara. The fossilized skull measures 20.86 inches (53 cm) in diameter, and the creature itself must have weighed about 2,200 lbs (1,000 kg)—about the size of a buffalo.

THE ARMADILLO *This is one of the very few mammals that has a protective shell. Its shell is made up of strips of hard material called scutes that are bound together by flesh. When threatened, the armadillo will roll up in a ball to protect its soft underbelly. It also digs very fast and sometimes can dig its way to safety. W. H. Hudson, an English traveler*

to Uruguay in the nineteenth century, described the armadillo as a "little old bent-backed gentleman in a rusty black coat trotting briskly about on some very important business." Female armadillos give birth to identical litters of males or females, like genetic clones.

THE TAMANDUÁ OR LESSER ANTEATER *This unusual-looking creature is a smaller cousin of the giant anteater, which is now extinct in Uruguay (but not in the world). The tamanduá spends about half its life in trees and is a very good climber. It has a prehensile tail that can grab and hold on to things like tree branches. Anteaters have large claws on their forefeet for self-defense and for breaking into insects' hiding places. They eat only insects but have no teeth to chew them with, so their hardy stomachs grind up the tough outer shells of insects like food processors.*

THE RHEA OR ÑANDÚ *This large ostrichlike bird stands 5 feet (1.5 m) tall and weighs about 50 pounds (23 kg). It cannot fly but is a very speedy runner. Rheas live in family groups of one male and many females. All the females will lay their eggs in one nest for the male to incubate. These birds have long been hunted for their hides and feathers, which are used as dusters.*

This distinctive Uruguayan ombú tree is some five hundred years old.

One of the most unusual trees in the country is the *ombú*, the bark of which is spongy and soft. Each ombú has its own unique shape. Its thick, twisting roots spread out over the ground. Some are over five hundred years old and can be 6 feet (2 m) in diameter. The ceibo tree (*Erythrina cristagalli*, not to be confused with the cieba tree) has beautiful scarlet flowers, which are the national flower of Uruguay. Palm trees grow along the southern shore. The rest of the country is covered with grasses and shrubs.

With so much water, both salt and fresh, there is an abundance of aquatic life. Freshwater fish include piranha, golden salmon, and pejerrey. Pacú, tararira, and surubí are similar to North American perch and bass. The Río de la Plata estuary is extremely rich in animal life. The fresh river water mingles with the warm ocean currents from Brazil and the colder ones from Argentina, giving the tidal estuary a mixture of fresh and salt waters. Sharks, rays, anchovies, and corvinas can be found in these waters.

The forests along the river and the lagoon marshes are home to dozens of species of birds. Some of the birds that live in wetlands are the royal duck, black-necked swan, creole duck, and various types of wild geese. The grasslands support partridges and the rhea, which resembles a smaller ostrich.

Many of Uruguay's original larger mammals, such as the jaguar, puma, collared peccary, and giant anteater, are no longer found there because of loss of habitat and overhunting. Among those that remain are the foxes; white-lipped peccaries; armadillos; capybaras; coatimundis, a type of raccoon; and anteaters. The Atlantic coast attracts a large colony of sea lions. They breed on Isla de Lobos, an island near Montevideo, and along the rocky eastern shore.

Over the centuries, Uruguay has gone by many names. When Europeans first came to this land in 1500, the first thing they named was the wide estuary where some of South America's major rivers empty into the Atlantic Ocean. This they perhaps erroneously named the Río de la Plata ("River of Silver"). There was no silver in the area, so historians speculate that the Spaniards named the river in hopes that it would lead to riches in the interior. Or maybe the waters simply looked silvery.

When Spain established a colony at the site of present-day Buenos Aires, they named the area of Argentina, Bolivia, Uruguay, and Paraguay the Viceroyalty of the Río de la Plata. During the colonial period, present-day Uruguay was known as the Banda Oriental, or the East Bank, because of its location east of the estuary. Uruguay struggled against Brazil from 1816 to 1820 before it was, in 1821, annexed to Brazil, whereupon it was called Cisplatine Province. Finally, in 1828, Uruguay gained its independence from Buenos Aires, Brazil, and Spain, and took the name República Oriental del Uruguay. The name Uruguay comes from the indigenous Guaraní language. It has been interpreted as meaning "river of painted birds" or "river of shells."

Legend has it that Montevideo was named by one of Ferdinand Magellan's crew in 1520. As the ship was sailing up the estuary, the lookout saw the conical hill of Montevideo and cried out "Monte vide eu" ("I see a mountain"). However, many historians and

linguists have rejected that explanation as unlikely for various reasons. Other explanations have been offered, but none are more than hypotheses.

During the nineteenth century, two factions fought for control of the new country. For thirteen years (1838–1851), one group laid siege to Montevideo, while the other defended it. During the war and afterward, the city was known as the Modern Troy because, like Troy of ancient Greece, it was forced to defend itself in a civil war.

This aerial view of downtown Montevideo shows the gardens of Plaza Independencia.

CITIES

MONTEVIDEO The biggest and most important city is Montevideo, the capital of Uruguay. With a population of approximately 1.7 million, it is home to nearly half of all the people in Uruguay, making it almost a city-state. It is located across the Río de la Plata from Buenos Aires, Argentina. Six of Uruguay's universities are in Montevideo, as are most of its television, radio, and newspaper headquarters. It is the seat of government, and more than two-thirds of Uruguay's industry is located in or near the capital.

Montevideo was founded in 1726 on a promontory near a large bay that forms a perfect natural harbor. It has gentle hills sloping to the sea. The main street runs along the back of a ridge of hills, the Cuchilla Grande. Across the bay from the Old City is the Cerro de Montevideo ("Lookout Mountain") or Montevideo Hill, which gave the city its name. Montevideo, considered one of the loveliest of cosmopolitan cities, is characterized by broad boulevards, parks, and stately buildings.

OTHER CITIES AND TOWNS The next largest cities in Uruguay are Salto (population about 104,000) and Paysandú (population about 113,000), both located along the Río Uruguay. Those cities have developed as a result of farming and trade with Argentina. Salto has benefited from the construction of a hydroelectric dam just north of the city, while Paysandú was given a huge boost by the construction of the General Artigas Bridge that connects Uruguay with Argentina.

The waterfront towns of Colonia del Sacramento and Punta del Este are both prime tourist destinations. Colonia del Sacramento, in the province of Colonia, was originally founded by Portuguese settlers in 1680 and is the oldest city in Uruguay. Punta del Este was founded in 1829 and was known as Villa Ituzaingó before its name was changed. The popular resort town attracts many local and foreign tourists during the summer and is growing steadily.

INTERNET LINKS

https://earthobservatory.nasa.gov/IOTD/view.php?id=4028
This NASA satellite image, with short explanation, shows the Rio de la Plata estuary, Montevideo, and Buenos Aires.

https://www.lonelyplanet.com/uruguay/montevideo
This travel site provides information and views of Uruguay, including Montevideo and other places of interest.

https://theculturetrip.com/south-america/uruguay/articles/20 -pictures-of-wonderful-animals-youll-find-in-uruguay
This photo gallery describes some of the common—and not so common—animals in Uruguay.

This 1887 engraved print shows a city street in Montevideo.

2

THE HISTORY OF URUGUAY HAS been affected by its geographic position between Argentina and Brazil. Nevertheless, Uruguay has maintained a distinct identity and for most of the twentieth century achieved unparalleled levels of education and well-being for its citizens.

BEFORE THE SPANISH

Uruguay is the only country in South America today that has no surviving indigenous people. The first archaeological evidence of human settlement in the area that was to become Uruguay is eight thousand years old. Those earliest inhabitants hunted animals and gathered plant and animal resources in order to survive. From around four thousand to eight thousand years ago, the stone tools these hunter-gatherers used became more sophisticated, and they also developed the use of the bow and arrow. By two thousand years ago, archaeological evidence suggests the existence of three distinct groups—the Chaná, the Guaraní, and the Charrúa. Those early peoples were all still present at the time of the European discovery of the territory in the 1500s.

THE CHANÁ were hunter-gatherers who supplemented their diet with fishing. They used the bow and arrow, and they smoked fish to preserve it. They moved about in small groups and were highly nomadic. Not

The European discovery and settlement of Uruguay forever changed the region's populace. Today it has no surviving indigenous groups and its population is mostly of European descent. Europeans remained in Uruguay for about three hundred years before José Gervasio Artigas began to agitate for independence, which was finally won in 1828.

Guarani people set fire to an enemy village in this nineteenth-century illustration of an imagined scene of Native life before European discovery.

much is known of the Chaná because they disappeared soon after the Spaniards started to settle in Uruguay.

THE GUARANÍ also made a quick exit from the area, but much more is known about their way of life because they are a large cultural group that still exists in other parts of South America.

The Guaraní were "shifting" cultivators. They planted crops in small garden plots in the forest, and they would periodically shift, or change fields, to avoid depleting the soil. They also hunted and gathered to supplement their diet. They grew corn, beans, cotton, and *yerba maté* (YAYR-bah mah-TAY). Maté, a tea made from the leaves and shoots of this shrub, is a stimulant containing caffeine. The beverage was later assimilated into the European culture of Uruguay.

The Guaraní arrived in the area of the Río de la Plata about two hundred years before the Europeans, and few survived the first colonial settlement.

THE CHARRÚA were also hunter-gatherers who used the bow and arrow. Unlike the Chaná, however, some of these people survived into the nineteenth century and played an important role in the wars of independence against Spain.

One of their most enduring legacies is the *bola* or *boleadora* (boh-lay-ah-DOR-ah), a weapon made of rocks that are attached to long leather thongs. The hunter swings the bola above his head (much like a cowboy twirling his lariat) and then releases it spinning through the air to wrap around the neck or legs of the hunted animal. The rocks would either kill the animal outright or at least hobble it. This device was adopted later by the Spaniards for rounding up horses and cattle on the open plains.

The Charrúa were able hunters and fighters and managed in part to survive by hunting as game the cattle introduced by the Spaniards in the 1600s. The last band of Charrúas was decimated at the Massacre of Salsipuedes in 1831.

DISAPPEARANCE OF THE INDIGENOUS POPULATION Historians have estimated that there were about nine thousand Charrúa and six thousand Chaná and Guaraní Indians at the time of contact with Europeans in the 1500s. By the time of independence, some three hundred years later, there

Guarani people harvest honey from hives in this eighteenth-century drawing by the Jesuit missionary Florian Baucke.

were only about five hundred Indians remaining in Uruguay. There were three main causes for the disintegration and disappearance of their cultures: disease, intentional extermination, and assimilation.

In the late 1500s and early 1600s, Europeans actually believed that the indigenous peoples of the New World were not fully human. Thus they set out to kill or enslave them. The original people in Uruguay were generally good fighters and were much more effective with their lances and arrows than the Spaniards were with their short-range, clumsy, and inaccurate guns. Disease was the cause of much of the decline in native populations throughout the Americas. Europeans unleashed many devastating diseases upon the New World, including influenza, syphilis, tuberculosis, and smallpox. With no immunity to these diseases, the original people were soon decimated. (The decline of the original peoples through diseases introduced by Europeans continues to this day, as the few remaining isolated indigenous groups of the Amazon jungle come into contact with outsiders.)

Finally, some Indians were herded into settlements run by religious groups. The goal of the priests was to convert them to Roman Catholicism and change their way of life. As most of Uruguay's original people were nomadic, they hated the confinement and rarely stayed long in those cramped places—in a sense, making them more vulnerable to being hunted down by other Spaniards.

EUROPEAN DISCOVERY AND SETTLEMENT

As early as 1502, Europeans had sighted Río de la Plata but did not explore the river farther. Then in 1515, the navigator and explorer Juan Díaz de Solís led an exploratory expedition of three ships and seventy men from Spain to South America. In 1516, having followed the eastern coast of South America southward, they thought they had found the southern tip of the continent when they reached the mouth of the Rio de la Plata. They landed about 70 miles (113 km) east of where Montevideo is now. After sailing up the Uruguay River, Solís and a landing party were immediately killed by a band of indigenous people, and promptly eaten in sight of the remaining crewmen on board the ship. Those crew members quickly abandoned the exploration

WORLD HERITAGE SITES

Since 1975, the United Nations Educational, Scientific and Cultural Organization (UNESCO) has maintained a list of international landmarks or regions considered to be of "outstanding value" to the people of the world. Such sites embody the common natural and cultural heritage of humanity, and therefore deserve particular protection. The organization works with the host country to establish plans for managing and conserving their sites. UNESCO also reports on sites which are in imminent or potential danger of destruction and can offer emergency funds to try to save the property.

The organization is continually assessing new sites for inclusion on the World Heritage list. In order to be selected, a site must be of "outstanding universal value" and meet at least one of ten criteria. These required elements include cultural value—that is, artistic, religious, or historical significance—and natural value, including exceptional beauty, unusual natural phenomenon, and scientific importance.

As of 2018, a total of 1073 sites have been listed, including 832 cultural, 206 natural, and 35 mixed properties in 167 nations. In Uruguay, there are two cultural sites, the Historic Quarter of the City of Colonia del Sacramento, pictured below, Uruguay's oldest town, and the Fray Bentos Industrial Landscape, or meat-packing district.

JOSÉ ARTIGAS, LEADER FOR INDEPENDENCE

José Gervasio Artigas was born in Montevideo in 1764. His family was prominent and wealthy, and he was educated by Franciscan friars. His experiences working with the gauchos, or ordinary cowboys, taught him to love the countryside and the common people.

He joined the fighting when the first independence movement flared up in Buenos Aires in 1810. He had his first military success against the forces loyal to Spain in 1811 at the Battle of Las Piedras. When a peace agreement was reached between independence fighters and Spanish loyalists in 1811, Artigas refused to abide by it because it implied that Uruguay would return to Spanish rule. He took his army on a long march away from Montevideo, called the Exodus of the Orientals (those from the east bank of the river). They were joined by 16,000 other patriots who supported his cause.

In 1813 he wrote a document known as "Instructions of Year 13," which outlined the principles of independence and confederation

A portrait of Jose Gervasio Artigas as shown on a Uruguayan Peso note.

for Uruguay. He eventually was forced to leave Uruguay when the Brazilians took over in 1820. Exiled to Paraguay, where he remained until his death in 1850, José Artigas is recognized as the father of Uruguayan independence.

and fled the region. Solís became known as the first European to set foot on Uruguayan land.

Throughout the 1500s, the Spaniards attempted to found settlements along various rivers but were repeatedly repelled by Indian attacks. In 1536, the explorer Pedro de Mendoza established the settlement of Buenos Aires on the western shore of the Río de la Plata, but the site was abandoned in 1541 after repeated attacks by the native people.

In 1580 the Spanish established a foothold with the second founding of Buenos Aires. In 1603 Governor Hernando Arias of Asunción, in present-day Paraguay, ordered that cattle and horses be released into the grasslands of Uruguay. The animals multiplied and attracted Buenos Aires ranchers, who crossed the river to capture the herds; but they never settled permanently on the Uruguayan side.

The City Gate of historic Colonia del Sacramento.

The Portuguese were the first people to be successful in settling Uruguay. They founded the city of Colonia del Sacramento along the Río de la Plata opposite Buenos Aires in 1680. In response to that, in 1726, the Spaniards founded Montevideo farther east along the estuary. By 1800, there were some ten thousand people in Montevideo and another twenty thousand in other parts of Uruguay. About one third of them were enslaved Africans.

INDEPENDENCE

The hero of the story of Uruguayan independence is General José Gervasio Artigas (1764—1850). He was the first to organize an army with the purpose of freeing Uruguay from Spain, Buenos Aires, and Brazilian interests. In 1810 fighting started in Buenos Aires between two factions—those who wanted Buenos Aires and all of Río de la Plata to sever ties to Spain and those who wanted to remain loyal to the Spanish crown.

General Artigas led the fight against the Spaniards with a ragtag band of Indians and ranchers, joining the revolt against the Spanish in 1810 and 1811. They successfully expelled the Spanish governor from Montevideo in 1814. Brazil decided to invade Uruguay, sensing that the newly liberated territory had been weakened by the revolution. In 1816 Artigas managed to repel a Brazilian attack, but by 1820 the Uruguayan general was defeated. He was exiled and the captured territory was named Cisplatine Province.

The fighting stopped for five years, during which time the British traded freely with the Brazilians for hides. In 1825 a group of thirty-three exiles from

THE MASSACRE AT SALSIPUEDES

Ironically, Salsipuedes (SAHL-see-poo-AY-days) means "Get out if you can" and is the name of the place where the last large group of Charrúa Indians were captured or killed outright by European Uruguayans.

After independence from Brazil in 1828, the new government decided that the Indians who had fought so bravely with General José Gervasio Artigas had to be destroyed. The excuse they used was that the Charrúa were stealing settlers' cattle.

The president at the time, General Fructuoso Rivera, was trusted by the Charrúa. In 1831 he sent them a message that they were needed by the army to defend the border against the Brazilians at Salsipuedes. When the loyal Indians arrived—some 340 men, women, and children—they set up camp, exchanged gifts with the army officers, and turned in for the night. The army of 1,200 soldiers attacked the group, killing forty Charrúa fighters outright and capturing the remaining 300. Those Charrúa were forced to march to Montevideo where they were enslaved as household servants. By 1840 there were only eighteen surviving Charrúa in Uruguay.

The Charrúa Indians no longer exist as a people. As of the 2001 Argentine census, there were only 676 persons of mixed blood with Charrúa ancestry living in Uruguay.

A memorial in Montevideo commemorates the last Charrúas.

Montevideo, led by Juan Antonio Lavalleja and aided by Argentina, invaded Cisplatine, and fighting for independence flared up again. With such renewed hostilities, the British could not trade in the area and so decided to intervene diplomatically.

The Brazilians and the Argentineans, with the help of British diplomacy, finally agreed to the establishment of an independent country between them. The new buffer state became known as the República Oriental del Uruguay and was granted its freedom in 1828. Lavalleja's group became known as the "Treinta y Tres Orientales" (Eastern Thirty-three) for the patriotic exiles' part in aiding the cause of Uruguayan freedom.

One of Uruguay's most famous paintings, *El Juramento de los Treinta y Tres Orientales* (Oath of the thirty-three Easterners), painted in 1877 by Juan Manuel Blanes, memorializes the 1825 event.

THE NINETEENTH CENTURY

This period was one of great internal political turmoil in Uruguay. The first constitution was established in 1830. General José Fructuoso Rivera, formerly a lieutenant in Artigas's army, became president of the new nation. In 1835 General Manuel Oribe succeeded Rivera as president. But in 1838,

Soldiers of Oribe's army are depicted in this watercolor.

Rivera deposed Oribe and took over Montevideo. Oribe sought help from Buenos Aires and came back to lay siege to Montevideo. From 1839 to 1851 the two forces fought over Montevideo in what became known as the Guerra Grande, or "Long War."

At one battle, the two sides each distinguished themselves with different colored hatbands—Oribe's forces wore white (*blanco*), while Rivera's wore red (*colorado*). Rivera's supporters tended to be urban-based and later formed a political party known as the Colorados, while Oribe's supporters were rural-based and formed the Partido Blanco.

From the end of the Long War until 1903—more than fifty years—the two hostile factions continued to fight and to struggle for the control of Uruguay's politics. At the end of the nineteenth century, after a series of conflicts and treaties, a system of sharing power between the two dominant parties was devised. That system, known as coparticipation, affected Uruguayan politics throughout the twentieth century.

Meanwhile, during the internal struggles of the Long War, Uruguay engaged in the Paraguayan War, also called the War of the Triple Alliance (1864—1870). Francisco Solano López, then the dictator of Paraguay, threatened Uruguayan independence, claiming he would take a port on the Río de la Plata for his country. In 1864 the Triple Alliance of Brazil, Argentina, and Uruguay went to war against Paraguay. The Paraguayans were outnumbered ten to one, and after six years of fighting, the Paraguayan population was virtually decimated. The war ended in 1870 with Paraguay totally defeated.

But politically, times were unsettled in Uruguay. Between 1870 and 1903, there were twenty-five different presidents. Of those, nine were forced out of power, two were assassinated, one suffered a grave injury, ten survived one or more attempted revolutions, and only three served problem-free.

THE BATLLE YEARS

José Batlle (bahj-jay) (1856—1929) was born into a strong Colorado Party family. His father, Lorenzo Batlle y Grau, served as president from 1868 to 1872. José Batlle himself founded a newspaper, *El Día*, in 1886 and wrote about politics throughout his life. He served as president during two periods, 1903—1907 and 1911—1915. During those eight years, he initiated far-reaching reforms that determined the future of Uruguay for more than sixty years. His legacy of political, social, and economic reform is known as *Batllismo* (bahj-JEES-moh).

José Batlle's image appears on a 1956 Uruguayan postage stamp.

President Batlle believed the Uruguayan economy was too small to be left in the hands of private interests, especially when such interests were foreign. So he began "autonomous entities," which were government-owned industries with monopolies over certain types of manufacturing or export goods. Since they were under the control of the government, these industries could be taxed according to need and the rights of workers would be protected.

He also believed that politics and religion should be separated; as a result, divorce became a purely civil matter. Among his more important reforms are the following: the abolition of income tax for low-paid public employees (1905); the establishment of secondary schools in every major city (1906); the right of women to sue for divorce on grounds of cruelty (1907); the establishment of state banks (1912); the creation of an autonomous agency to run the port of Montevideo (1912); the nationalization of the telephone utility (1915); the provision of credit to the rural poor through state banks; and the drafting of a new constitution. The constitution was adopted after his second term in 1919.

Perhaps Batlle's most enduring legacy was a system of government he created called the *colegiado* (koh-lay-hee-AH-doh), or collegium system. Between 1907 and 1911, he traveled extensively in Europe, and was most impressed with the Swiss system of government in which there is no single president but rather a panel of citizens with equal authority in control of the executive. He supported the creation of a new constitution that divided the powers of government between the president and a nine-member collegium with six representatives from the party that won the elections and three from the losing party. In a sense, that was a continuation of the nineteenth-century struggle for coparticipation between the two big political parties. The new constitution also guaranteed the secret ballot and a system of voting called "double simultaneous balloting." Most of the other politicians of the time rejected the collegial idea, but when Batlle threatened to run for the presidency a third time if they did not pass the constitution, they agreed to accept the concept.

Democracy, loosely defined, was maintained throughout that period, but competition for control of the collegium and efforts to abolish it by both parties continued. During the Great Depression (1930s), there was a brief suspension of elections while two factions, one from each party, tried to control the government. With large increases in exports resulting from the Korean War (1950—1953), however, democracy was revived. Uruguay had one of the most stable regimes in Latin America throughout the first half of the twentieth century. All that serenity was to change in the 1960s.

REPRESSION AND DICTATORSHIP

Although Batllismo had created a relatively stable government with an educated population protected by a large social welfare system, it also left a legacy of extravagant government spending. When the export economy was booming, that deep pocket worked fine, but when there were slowdowns in the demand for Uruguay's main exports (beef, hides, and wool), the government was left with huge expenditures and little income. That meant heavy borrowing, resulting in inflation. The cost of living for Uruguayans doubled between 1959 and 1962, doubling again between 1962 and 1964. Inflation skyrocketed to 100 percent by 1965. People wanted change, starting with the collegial system.

The Colorados won the election of 1967 under General Oscar Gestido, who soon abolished the collegium and awarded more powers to himself as the president. When Gestido died later that same year, his vice president, Areco Pacheco, took power and began to outlaw various left-wing groups, newspapers, and small political parties that had sprung up in response to the economic crisis.

Repression and suspension of civil rights continued and intensified in the late 1960s in reaction to a newly formed revolutionary group called the Tupamaros. That group began an armed struggle against the government, believing it was selling out Uruguay to foreign interests at the cost of Uruguayans' well-being. They were responsible for many acts of terrorism, but the two most notable were the kidnappings of Daniel Mitrione, an American, in 1970, and Geoffrey Jackson, the British ambassador, in 1971.

While most Uruguayans did not want violence, there was a growing sense that a new political party was needed to represent the people. In the 1971 election, a new group called the Frente Amplio ("Broad Front") ran for power. This was a coalition of left-wing political groups headed by Liber Seregi. To the shock and dismay of the other two more conservative parties, the Frente Amplio took 30 percent of the vote in Montevideo and 18 percent of the national vote. Juan María Bordaberry of the Colorados was sworn in as president in 1972, but many voters suspected fraud.

During the whole period of government repression, the military had been quietly growing in strength and power and was increasing its pressure on the president to do things its way. For the first two years of Bordaberry's presidency, the military stayed in the wings trying to control him indirectly, but in 1973 it lost its patience and, in a coup, deposed Bordaberry and established a dictatorship. The main causes for the military takeover were economic decline, social unrest among workers and students, terrorism wielded by the Tupamaros, and weak and ineffective politicians. By 1973 the military had effectively wiped out the Tupamaros, but it continued to target them as an excuse to justify their rampant abuse of civil rights.

During the dictatorship, the number of military and police personnel nearly doubled to an all-time high of 64,000 in 1978, and they were used to keep Uruguayans in a state of constant fear through grave human rights abuses. As a result, 10 percent of Uruguayans left the country, never to return.

THE MUSEUM OF MEMORY

During the twelve years of the dictatorship, some 180 Uruguayans were killed by government forces—most of them outside of Uruguay itself, and many in Argentina. The military, police, and intelligence forces of Uruguay had formed a secret alliance with other dictatorships in Argentina, Bolivia, Brazil, Chile, and Paraguay called Operation Condor. Each nation exchanged intelligence with its counterparts in neighboring countries and kidnapped, tortured, and killed activists from those countries on behalf of its allies. Many of the dead were never found, and are among the "disappeared" (desaparecidos). In Uruguay, more than five thousand people were arrested for political reasons, and almost 10 percent of the citizens emigrated from the country.

In 2007, the Museum of Memory, or Museo de la Memoria (MUME), opened in Montevideo. Dedicated to the memory of state terrorism and the struggle of the Uruguayan people against the dictatorship, the museum hosts permanent and temporary exhibitions. It also sponsors courses, seminars, and other educational activities.

The education system was virtually dismantled; 80 percent of university professors and 40—50 percent of public school teachers were arrested, fired, or fled their jobs in fear of torture.

One of the goals of the military government was to improve Uruguay's economy. Unfortunately, it came into power just as the worldwide oil crisis started in 1973, when the oil-producing nations decided to raise the price of gas and oil. Every country dependent on imported oil suffered during that time, and those with their own oil industry tried to generate more money by protecting it through trade tariffs.

The Uruguayan military thought it could stimulate the economy by opening it to foreign investment. That only made things worse, as small Uruguayan companies could not compete and went under. Government spending on social programs was cut and wages were frozen, which increased poverty. Continued loss of income from falling exports resulted in heavy borrowing from international banks; by 1981 Uruguay's debt was $4 billion. With a population of only 3 million, that sum was staggering!

RETURN TO DEMOCRACY

The end of military rule began in 1980 with the failure of a referendum organized by the military that would have guaranteed their continued power. Elections were promised for 1984, though the military still insisted that certain left-wing parties could not participate. Faced with worsening economic conditions and massive public demonstrations, however, the military reluctantly gave back power and responsibility to civilian leaders. Eventually the three main parties and the military agreed on a new constitution, and elections were held in 1984 as planned.

President Julio Maria Sanguinetti is photographed at a press conference in 1988.

The presidential election of 1984 was won by the Colorado Battlista candidate, Julio María Sanguinetti, who had gained power only on the sufferance of the generals. Against popular demands for criminal trials and retribution, Sanguinetti granted the military a blanket amnesty for their human rights abuses of the previous eleven years.

The challenges for subsequent democratic governments were to revive an economy suffering from an incredible debt burden and vocal labor unrest; to rebuild the education system after years of neglect; to mediate between the military and groups who want to see them tried and jailed for their crimes; and to continue to support a large military budget to prevent another coup.

In 1989 the Blanco Party returned to power. Five years later, however, in 1994, Julio María Sanguinetti, of the Colorado Battlista, won a second term. The margin was extremely narrow, with Sanguinetti taking 31.40 percent of the votes, followed by Alberto Volonte with 30.20 percent, Tabaré Vázquez with 30.02 percent, and Rafael Michelini with 5.04 percent. The result was a coalition government that reflected the wish of the Uruguayans to return to their traditional democracy.

TWENTY-FIRST CENTURY

Uruguay's first leftist president, Tabaré Vázquez, a cancer specialist, took office in 2005. The coalition he led, the Broad Front (Frente Amplio), also called the Progressive Encounter (Encuentro Progresista), was composed of former guerrillas, socialists, communists, and independent leftists. He won on the promise to improve a stagnant economy, bring greater social justice to Uruguay, and deal with the legacy of human rights violations during the 1973—1985 military dictatorship.

President Tabaré Vázquez greets supporters following his first term election in 2005.

The Vázquez administration made good on this promise and uncovered important forensic evidence of prior abuses during his first three years in office. One of his first acts as president was to announce a $100-million-a-year National Emergency Plan to assist the estimated 20 percent of Uruguayans mired in abject poverty.

In 2006, the former president-turned-dictator Juan Maria Bordaberry and his former foreign minister were arrested in connection with the 1976 killings of four political opponents. He and former military ruler Gregorio Alvarez were eventually found guilty of murder and other human rights abuses during their time in office, and sentenced to prison. Because of his advanced age, Bordaberry served his term at home and died shortly thereafter, in 2011.

Also in 2011, under President José Mujica, who had been elected in 2010, the Uruguayan Congress annulled the amnesty law that had protected members of the military from the dictatorship era from being held accountable for human rights abuses. Mujica himself had been imprisoned by the military dictatorship during those years. Since Uruguayan presidents cannot serve consecutive terms, in 2015, when Mujica's term ended, the popular former president Tabaré Vázquez was elected to another term.

President José Mujica talks to reporters in 2010.

INTERNET LINKS

http://news.bbc.co.uk/2/hi/americas/country_profiles/1229362.stm
This BBC News timeline provides important dates in the history of Uruguay.

https://whc.unesco.org/en/statesparties/uy
Links to Uruguay's two World Heritage Sites are found on this UNESCO website.

GOVERNMENT

Farmers and other laborers wave Uruguayan flags during a
demonstration for tax relief in January 2018.

3

F OR MOST OF THE TWENTIETH century, Uruguay maintained a consistently democratic governmental system with two traditional parties. Since the military dictatorship collapse in the 1980s and the subsequent return to democracy, the nation has shouldered many difficulties and new parties have emerged to challenge the traditional leadership.

The military has remained relatively strong since its dictatorship succumbed, but it is now subject to presidential control through the minister of defense. Military service is voluntary, in any of the three branches of the service: army, navy, and air force.

THE CONSTITUTION

The country's first constitution was adopted in 1830. The one now in use is the nation's sixth constitution, which was adopted in 1967, and has been amended several times.

During the civic-military dictatorship of 1973—1985, the military essentially suspended the constitution. In 1976, it added a series of constitutional decrees that significantly changed the form of government. In 1980, it proposed a new constitution that would have provided for a strong, continuing role for the military, and which would

The Palacio Legislativo (Parliament Building) in Montevideo.

continue the 1976 constitutional decrees. However, the Uruguayan people rejected that version in a referendum. Nevertheless, the military instituted some of the proposed changes anyway.

Once civilian rule resumed in 1985, the constitution of 1967 was reinstated. Since then, it has been amended four times, most recently in 2004, when 64.7 percent of Uruguayan people voted to make the right to water a constitutional human right. In 2014, a constitutional referendum was held to propose an amendment to Article 43 of the constitution, which would have lowered the age of criminal responsibility from eighteen to sixteen. The voters rejected the proposal by a narrow margin.

STRUCTURE OF GOVERNMENT

EXECUTIVE BRANCH Uruguay is a constitutional republic. The president is the chief of state and head of government, and he is aided by a vice president and a council of ministers appointed by the president with approval of the General Assembly. Both the president and vice president are elected by popular vote for five-year terms and may not serve consecutive terms. They may, however, serve again in a nonconsecutive term, which is what President Tabaré Vásquez did when he won a second term in 2015.

The Council of Ministers (the cabinet) is appointed by the president with approval by the General Assembly. The ministers oversee ten departments: the interior; foreign affairs; economy and finance; transportation and public works; health; labor and social security; livestock, agriculture, and fisheries; education and culture; defense; industry, energy, and mining; tourism; and territorial regulation and environment.

LEGISLATIVE BRANCH a bicameral General Assembly (Asamblea General) provides checks and balances on the president's authority. The Chamber of Senators (Cámara de Senadores) consists of thirty-one members—thirty elected representatives headed by the vice president; and the Chamber of Representatives (Cámara de Representantes) consists of ninety-nine elected representatives.

The country is divided into nineteen departments (administrative subdivisions), each with an elected governor. Uruguay's departments are not like states, since their autonomy is quite limited. Most decisions are made by the national government.

Senators discuss legalizing marijuana in 2013.

THE URUGUAYAN FLAG

The flag of Uruguay was designed and approved in 1830. There are four blue stripes alternating with five white ones. Those are the colors of Argentina and symbolize Uruguay's connection with Buenos Aires during colonial times. There is also a white patch with the Sun of May (sun with a face) emblazoned in gold upon it. The Sun of May has sixteen rays that are alternately straight and wavy, symbolizing independence from their Spanish overlords in May 1810. The Sun of May is a symbol in both Argentina and Uruguay, and represents Inti, the sun god of the Incas. The flag's design is said to have been influenced by the style of the American flag.

JUDICIAL BRANCH There are five judges on the Supreme Court of Justice, who are chosen by the executive branch and serve for ten-year terms. They may be reappointed after a break of five years. The Supreme Court appoints all other judges in the country. There are also the courts of appeal, district courts, peace courts, and rural courts.

THE ELECTORAL PROCESS

A person may be elected president only if he or she has not served in that position for at least three months prior to the election. This serves to prevent an incumbent and his party from taking over the position for life. Elections are held every five years, and all government positions are elected simultaneously and proportionally. Everyone over eighteen years of age is eligible to vote.

The Uruguayan constitution provides for direct public participation in governmental decisions. If ordinary citizens are unhappy with a decision, they can force the government to hold a national referendum to resolve it. That means that the troubling issue is put to all voters to decide. To do that, 25 percent of eligible voters must first sign a petition requesting the referendum. Once that is accomplished, the government must then hold the vote within sixty days and abide by the results.

POLITICAL PARTIES

Uruguay has a multiparty political system with three main players in modern elections—the National Party; the Colorado Party, which has held the presidency almost continuously since independence; and the Frente Amplio (Broad Front), which has emerged as a coalition of progressive and radical left-wing groups.

The right-wing conservative Blanco Party, which is now known as the National Party, was formed under General Manuel Oribe in the nineteenth century. It tends to represent the rural and conservative elements of the population. Although it is considered the second largest party and the traditional opponent of the Colorados, its candidates have held the presidency only three times since Uruguay's independence from Brazil.

The moderate Colorado (Red) Party tends to represent the urban middle class, which is the largest group in Uruguay. José Batlle shaped the party into a mature political organ, but his radical reforms also split the party into factions. Some of his party members supported his ideas of a collegial system, while others did not. Although the collegial system has long been abandoned in Uruguay, those egalitarian factions in the Colorado Party still exist.

The Frente Amplio or Broad Front, a party made up of a coalition of many smaller parties and party factions, was formed in 1971 to oppose increasing repression by the government. In the 1971 election, the Frente Amplio won 18.3 percent of the vote, but once the military took power, the party was outlawed. The Frente leaders were jailed or went into exile during the dictatorship. When democracy returned in 1984, Frente Amplio won 21.3 percent of the popular vote, demonstrating that its support was growing.

PRESIDENT TABARÉ VÁZQUEZ

Tabaré Ramón Vázquez Rosas (b. 1940), from the Broad Front coalition, first served as Uruguay's head of state from 2005–2010. His first victory coincided with a regional trend toward left-wing governments in Brazil, Venezuela, Chile, and Argentina, and he was the first leftist president in Uruguay's history.

Bolstered by the country's robust economic growth over the last decade, as well as by the popularity of the previous leftist President José Mujica, Vázquez won a second nonconsecutive term again in 2014. He defeated the much younger National Party candidate Luis Lacalle Pou by a tally of 56.5 percent to 43.4 percent.

Vázquez, a cancer specialist doctor and also a former mayor of Montevideo, promised to alleviate poverty. On taking office, he announced a $200 million emergency plan to help the poor. He also oversaw a program to provide laptop computers to all primary school children in the country.

Although Vázquez is politically more moderate than Mujica, the man he replaced in 2014, his election is seen as a sign of the popular desire for continuity.

The party is quite left-wing, including communists, socialists, Christian Democrats, and radical splinter groups from the two major parties.

The Communist Party became an official party in 1921 and has always been considered very radical. Its members were founding members of the Frente Amplio in 1971. During the dictatorship and its first election, the Communist Party was outlawed. The government did recognize it in 1985, and in the 1989 election the communists won about 10 percent of the vote.

The socialists were organized as a party in 1910, but in 1921 a majority of the members broke away to form the more radical Communist Party. Throughout the twentieth century, the socialists became increasingly left-wing, opposing foreign investment in Uruguay, for example. Some members of the Socialist Party helped form the Tupamaros, the armed guerrilla group. The socialists and communists are now part of the Frente Amplio coalition.

Finally, there is the Christian Democratic Party, the first Roman Catholic political party in Uruguay. It was founded in 1910. Traditionally, it has not received more than 3—5 percent of the vote. It's now part of the Frente Amplio.

INTERNET LINKS

https://www.aljazeera.com/indepth/opinion/2013/06/20136188352149830.html
This opinion piece argues that Uruguay's government should establish a national day of remembrance to confront the history of the civic-military dictatorship that ruled from 1973 to 1985.

https://www.constituteproject.org/constitution/Uruguay_2004.pdf
The current Uruguayan constitution is available here in English.

https://www.nytimes.com/2016/02/10/opinion/uruguays-quiet-democratic-miracle.html
In this opinion piece, the author explains why Uruguay's democracy works.

ECONOMY

A portrait of the artist Pedro Figari is visible on the 200-peso note among an array of Uruguayan banknotes.

4

URUGUAY HAS A FREE MARKET economy supported by a stable democracy and a well-educated workforce. Its pro-market policies are balanced by a strong social safety net, financed by high taxes. The economy relies heavily on agricultural exports such as milk, beef, rice, and wool, and is subject to periodic swings in international demand for those products.

Along with Bolivia and Paraguay, Uruguay has a special geographic and historical position as a buffer between Argentina and Brazil. Those two countries are giants in physical size, population, and economic production, while Uruguay has very few natural resources. It does not have large forests or mines, and much of its land is unsuited to growing crops.

For that reason, the original settlers turned to livestock production, which is a very significant part of the economy even today. Uruguay's population is too small to support a big industrial sector. All these factors have made it difficult for Uruguay to sustain economic growth.

In addition, Uruguay generally imports more goods such as cars and machinery from Brazil and Argentina than it exports food to them. That

Political strife in the early years of Uruguay's independence caused great economic instability. Now, in general, the economy is doing well. Uruguay's main exports are in livestock and agricultural products and their related goods. The country is also part of a South American free trade bloc called Mercosur.

WHAT IS GDP?

Gross domestic product (GDP) is a measure of a country's total production. The number reflects the total value of goods and services produced over one year. Economists use it to determine whether a country's economy is growing or contracting. Growth is good, while a falling GDP means trouble. Dividing the GDP by the number of people in the country determines the GDP per capita (per person). This number provides an indication of a country's average standard of living—the higher the better.

In 2017, the GDP per capita in Uruguay was approximately $22,400—number 84 out of 230 countries. (For comparison, the GDP per capita in the United States for that year was $57,400, at number 20.)

results in trade deficits because the country is losing money by having to spend more on imports than it earns from exports. From 1999 to 2002 the economy suffered a major setback when Argentina made large withdrawals of US dollars deposited in Uruguayan banks. This led to a nosedive of the Uruguayan peso and a massive rise in unemployment to 19.4 percent. Just as the country was picking up speed from that setback, the international global financial crisis of 2008—2009 slowed Uruguay's growth once again. Economic growth has been on the upswing since then.

Since Batlle's reforms at the beginning of the twentieth century (except for the period of military dictatorship), the government has tried to provide its people with a good education at a reasonable cost and other welfare benefits, such as wage protection and social security for retired people.

CURRENCY

The currency in Uruguay is called the peso Uruguayo, or Uruguayan peso. It is divided into one hundred centésimos, or cents. Because of inflation and soaring prices, in 1993 the currency was changed, so that one thousand of the old pesos became one new peso. With the new currency, prices were affordable again and the currency was stronger on the international market. In 2018, one US dollar was worth about 28.27 Uruguayan pesos.

MAIN INDUSTRIES

AGRICULTURE   About 13 percent of the country's labor force works in the agricultural sector, which, in turn, provides about 6.2 percent of the total GDP. Agricultural products are the primary source of exports. About 41 million acres (16.6 million hectares) of land are devoted to agriculture, and approximately 90 percent of that land is used to raise animals that provide meat and dairy products, wool, hides, and leather goods. In 2016, Uruguay had some 6.5 million sheep (an unusually fierce storm in 2013 killed more than 30,000 sheep) and 12 million head of cattle. The nation also produces rice, wheat, soybeans, and barley as well as peaches, oranges, tangerines, and pears.

There are three agricultural zones in the country: the southern zone, which produces fruit and vegetables for consumers living in Montevideo and for export; the northern zone, where the sheep and cattle ranches are situated; and the eastern zone, where grains and cereals are grown.

A modern-day gaucho drives a herd of cattle into a corral in Tacuarembo, Uruguay.

Workers converse at a canned meat factory in Fray Bentos.

Other economic activity includes mining of semiprecious stones such as amethyst and topaz, fishing, hydroelectric power production, and forestry.

MANUFACTURING Although agriculture accounts for most exports, manufacturing and construction contribute 25 percent of the country's total income in a given year. The main manufacturing industries are meatpacking, oil refining, manufacturing of cement, food and beverage processing, leather and cloth manufacturing, and chemical processing. Still, manufacturing depends on farming, since many of the factories process food or produce clothing made from wool and leather.

MERCOSUR

In 1991 a new trade bloc was created including Uruguay, Paraguay, Brazil, and Argentina. Mercosur, commonly called Mercado Común del Cono Sur, or the Southern Market, is a free-trade agreement wherein participating countries trade with one another without charging any taxes on imports and exports.

At the time, the charter members hoped to form a common economic market similar to that of the European Union (EU), and even considered introducing a common currency. Given that all four of the countries had emerged from dictatorships in the 1980s, the group was committed to democracy. Venezuela joined Mercosur in 2012 but was indefinitely suspended in 2016 for failing to comply with the group's democratic standards.

In 2017, Mercosur's four founding members had a combined GDP of roughly $2.9 trillion, making it one of the world's largest economic blocs. However, some economic observers have expressed concern about its future, suggesting that political fractures could tear the group apart. Meanwhile, in 2016 Mercosur revived previously stalled negotiations with the EU—which itself was reeling from the recent vote in Great Britain to leave the union (Brexit)—and was looking to begin trade talks with Canada, Australia, and New Zealand.

SERVICE SECTOR The lion's share of the national economy is generated by the service sector. That includes businesses such as restaurants, hotels, transportation, community services, communications, and any other service that people pay for in daily life—a haircut or housecleaning. One of the services Uruguay offers to the world is its special banking system. Banks in Uruguay, like those in Switzerland, keep all accounts completely private; no one can find out who has money in them or how much they have. The service sector accounts for about 68.8 percent of the country's total income every year.

INTERNATIONAL TRADE

Uruguay's primary trade partners are China, Brazil, Argentina, the United States, and Germany. The biggest export commodities are live

animals and animal products such as milk, meat, fish, furs, wool, woolen cloth and clothing, and hides and leather products; also rice, vegetables, processed food and drinks. The main imports from the partner countries include machinery, vehicles, fuels such as oil and gas, and chemicals. Uruguay's position as primarily an agricultural country with few natural resources of its own is reflected in its trade.

Shipping containers are loaded in the port district of Montevideo.

ENERGY, TRANSPORTATION, COMMUNICATIONS

Virtually all urban dwellers and nearly 94 percent of the rural population have access to electricity. Uruguay generates hydroelectric power from dams on its many rivers—about 35 percent of its electricity comes from this source. One of the largest dams is at Salto Grande on the Río Uruguay. Uruguay produces no crude oil or natural gas and needs to import petroleum products from Argentina to supplement its energy supply, particularly for transportation needs. The imported crude oil is then refined into usable forms in Uruguay. There are no nuclear reactors in the country.

In recent years, an investment in wind power and other renewable sources transformed the country's electricity production such that in 2015, nearly 95 percent of its generation came from clean energy sources, including from hydropower, biomass, and wind energy.

Uruguay has one of the best highway systems in all of South America. Of the 48,000 miles (77,249 km) of roads, some 90 percent are rural dirt roads; the rest are paved or graveled. The railway system is owned by the government and is used primarily for transporting goods rather than people. The principal shipping ports are Montevideo, Punta del Este, Colonia, Fray Bentos, Paysandú, and Salto. There are two international airports: Montevideo and Punta del Este. For travel within the country, there are seven smaller airports with permanent runways, and more than one hundred others with unpaved runways.

Most telecommunications facilities are centered in Montevideo, where the majority of the people live. With over one million landline telephones and five million cellular phones in operation, Uruguay has one of the highest number of telephones per capita in South America.

INTERNET LINKS

https://www.cfr.org/backgrounder/mercosur-south-americas -fractious-trade-bloc
The Council on Foreign Relations provides a good explanation of Mercosur.

https://www.cia.gov/library/publications/the-world-factbook /geos/uy.html
The *CIA World Factbook* provides up-to-date information on Uruguay's economy, communications, transportation, and energy profiles.

https://www.heritage.org/index/country/uruguay
The country's Index of Economic Freedom ranking can be found on this site.

http://www.worldbank.org/en/country/uruguay/overview
This site gives a quick overview of Uruguay's economic situation.

ENVIRONMENT

Argentinean activists protest a potentially pollution-causing paper mill on the Uruguay River in 2010.

5

U RUGUAY IS ONE OF THE LEAST polluted countries in South America. Expanding city populations and industries, however, have resulted in environmental problems such as compromised clean water sources, inefficient waste disposal, and destruction of natural habitats. In the rural areas, extensive cattle ranching has had a deleterious effect on the natural savanna lands.

Deep beneath much of Uruguay is the famous underground Guarano Aquifer (Acuífero Guarani), the second-largest known freshwater reservoir in the world. It stretches under Brazil, Paraguay, and Argentina.

Brown cows are penned at one of Uruguay's many large cattle farms.

WATER AND SANITATION

Water quality in Uruguay has been among the best in South America. Almost 100 percent of the population, urban and rural, has access to safe drinking water. Almost as many have access to sanitation facilities. Still, recent economic growth has threatened Uruguay's overall water quality. The Santa Lucia River, which provides more than 60 percent of the population with tap water, has become more polluted.

Part of the problem can be traced to an increase of industrial waste products from agricultural companies being released into the sanitation system. The toxic effluent finds its way into surface and ground water. In times of drought, a lack of rainfall causes the toxins to build up. In addition, excessive amounts of fertilizers and pesticides washing into the lakes and rivers bring about an imbalance in the ecosystem, triggering a process called eutrophication. The water becomes too rich with nutrients, inducing the growth of cyanobacteria, which clog water filters in treatment plants, produce toxins, and result in the death of aquatic animal life from a lack of oxygen.

The National Environment Office of Uruguay's Ministry of Environment monitors the rivers is working to clean up the Santa Lucia River, but the project could take decades.

Another source of substantial pollution and agitation is acid rain from Brazilian industry. Up to one-fifth of the country is affected by acid rain generated in Uruguay's northern neighbor, Brazil.

AIR POLLUTION

Air pollution is not a big problem in Uruguay, but there is room to improve the air quality, and the government is paying attention to the matter. Uruguay's air emissions inventory shows that the main contribution to particulate matter emissions comes from residential use of wood stoves for heating and cooking, particularly in the densely populated municipal region of Montevideo.

HABITAT DESTRUCTION

Unique grasslands, palm savannas, and gallery forests once covered the entire country of Uruguay. However, cattle ranching and agriculture caused tremendous changes to the ecology of these lands; today there are only small patches of intact native habitat remaining. Overgrazing has destroyed or degraded the natural vegetation and the introduction of alien species—both plant and animal—have crowded out the native species. A number of species have already become extinct in the country, including the giant anteater and the jaguar.

The Uruguayan government is acting to preserve what remains of the native flora in this ecoregion. However, the historic dominance and economic importance of cattle ranching leaves little hope that much will be accomplished.

INTERNET LINKS

**https://www.theguardian.com/environment/2015/dec/03/uruguay
-makes-dramatic-shift-to-nearly-95-clean-energy**
This article examines Uruguay's impressive growth of clean energy.

https://www.worldwildlife.org/ecoregions/nt0710
This blistering report on the critical state of Uruguay's savanna details the damage done to its environment.

URUGUAYANS

A woman bikes beside Pocitos Beach in Montevideo.

6

O N THE ONE HAND, URUGUAY IS SAID to be a "melting pot" of many ethnicities. Indeed, various waves of immigration from Europe brought people of Spanish, Italian, and German origins to this relatively small country. Descendants of enslaved Africans provide a racial component to the mix, and tiny numbers of people from other parts of the world can be found here. But the melting pot is not really all that varied, as white people of European origins greatly dominate the population and the culture.

Compared to other South American countries, Uruguay has a largely European-descended white population, a small mixed-race population, and very few people of indigenous origins.

The indigenous people are noticeably missing. Many reports claim the native people disappeared over the course of historic massacres by the white settlers, which is essentially true. The Charrúa people, for example, are said to have died out in 1831, following the genocidal Massacre of Salsipuedes.

However, some people of Charrúa descent are emerging among today's Uruguayans to reclaim their identity and heritage. The Consejo de la Nación Charrúa (Council of the Charrúan Nation, or CONACHA) was formed in 2005 to that purpose.

People enjoy the sunshine in a waterfront park.

ETHNIC GROUPS

Uruguay has one of the most homogeneous populations in South America. The majority—88 percent of the population—are descendants of European settlers. There are two main groups—those whose forebears were from Spain and those whose ancestors originally came from Italy. Both groups now speak Spanish and intermingle everywhere.

The next largest ethnic group is the *mestizos*, the mixed race descendants of unions between Indians and Spaniards and Italians during colonial times. Mestizos make up 8 percent of the population and generally live in rural areas.

Finally, 4 percent of the population is of African descent. Most are descended from enslaved people taken from Africa in the eighteenth and early nineteenth centuries. They live mostly in Montevideo where the largest concentration of slave-holding people lived. Some members of that African-Uruguayan group, however, came to Uruguay from Brazil, and they tend to live along the northern border with Brazil.

Though Uruguay is an open and tolerant society, some racism persists among different ethnic groups.

THE SLAVE TRADE

The slave trade had been in existence for some time when the Spanish crown made it legal in 1791. At that time, Montevideo was designated the official slave-trading port for the Río de la Plata area. Many ships came bringing Africans who had been taken forcefully from their homes and shipped as cargo to the New World to be sold.

Despite their debased social position, African Uruguayans participated in all the major wars of the nineteenth century, including the independence movement when they fought with General José Artigas. The first step to end slavery came in 1825 when trading for new slaves was prohibited and all slaves born in Uruguay were given their freedom. There were other laws aimed at ending slavery, but it was not until 1853 that all African Uruguayans finally gained their freedom.

IMMIGRATION, MIGRATION, EMIGRATION

As in many New World nations, the bulk of the modern Uruguayan population is descended from immigrants from all over the world. First were the Spaniards, who started settling in Uruguay in the eighteenth century. The next group to arrive were enslaved Africans, who were used mostly as domestic servants. After abolition, the Africans stayed on to form a small but vital subculture in the country. Argentina was in need of immigrants and sent agents to Italy to recruit settlers. But some of those people ended up in Uruguay. In 1890 the Uruguayan government actively encouraged immigration by promising able-bodied arrivals food and shelter for eight days after landing and free transportation to the interior of the country. Consequently, many people who originally planned to go to Argentina ended up in Uruguay instead.

European migration to Uruguay has changed through the years. Originally, under Spanish colonialism, only Spanish settlers were encouraged to move to the New World. After independence, however, the new government realized that many more people were needed to settle the interior and develop the country. From 1830 to 1870, there was a boom in European migration, with Spanish, French, and Italians making up large immigrant groups. In 1860 it

An aerial view shows the dense highrises of the capital city.

was estimated that 48 percent of the population was foreign-born. Nearer the turn of the twentieth century, Italians had become the largest group of new immigrants.

The last wave of European immigrants began arriving at the start of the century and did not subside until the 1930s. Most of those immigrants were Jews from parts of Europe where their religion was not tolerated. Some were Spanish and Portuguese Jews, but in the 1930s the majority were from Germany. Immigration has slowed down dramatically since the 1950s.

Once in Uruguay, most immigrants chose to live in and around Montevideo and other large urban centers. More than half of the total population lives in Montevideo and in the neighboring department of Canelones. The general pattern is that those born in small villages move to the capital city of their department to look for work, while those born in the department capitals tend to move to Montevideo. With so few people left to look after the countryside, Uruguay is almost a city-state.

There has also been a steady pattern of emigration—residents leaving the country. The emigration of the young and educated started when the country began to experience serious economic problems in the 1960s and continued during the military dictatorship in the 1970s. Official figures suggest that 180,000 Uruguayans departed for good in the period 1963—1975. The peak of outward migration was in 1973—1975: 30,000 left in 1973, 60,000 in 1974, and nearly 40,000 in 1975. For the duration of the dictatorship, 1975—1985, another 150,000 Uruguayans left the country. Between 1996 and 2002, almost 100,000 skilled workers, 3 percent of the entire population, emigrated during a lengthy recession.

An airport building is lit up in this night view of Montevideo's Carrasco International Airport.

Although most emigrants went to Argentina, where they could blend in easily, the United States, Australia, Spain, Brazil, and Venezuela were also popular destinations. When Julio María Sanguinetti became the first democratically elected president in 1984, he invited all exiles and migrants back. But only a handful returned. Many who visited shortly after the election were so shocked by the poor state of the country that they decided never to return.

AN AGING POPULATION

Uruguay has an unusual demographic pattern. With the slowdown in immigration halfway through the twentieth century and acceleration in emigration, Uruguay lost and could not replace its youth. The average age of the population increased as the arrival of young immigrants declined. It increased even more in the 1960s and 1970s when young people fled by the thousands to escape the country's repressive junta, or dictatorship. Another

A family of several generations takes a walk together.

100,000 young and highly qualified Uruguayans left during the country's lengthy and deep recession between 1995 and 2002 for greener pastures in Europe and the United States. That is one reason why Uruguay has the highest proportion of elderly people in all South America, with about 14.25 percent of its people aged sixty-five or older in 2017.

The trend was widened even more by changes in the birth and death rates in the twentieth century. Advances in medicine made it possible for people to live longer, and the introduction of birth control methods made it possible for families to have fewer children. When both the birthrate and the death rate decrease, the average age of the population increases, as young people grow up and fewer children are born. By contrast, most other South American countries have the reverse problem of huge populations under the age of fifteen due to high birth and low death rates. Uruguay is more like North American countries in its demographics than it is like its neighbors.

SOCIAL CLASSES

Uruguay is unlike its neighbors in terms of its class system, too. Although there are rich people and poor people, the country has a large middle class. Roughly 5 percent of the population can be considered extremely wealthy, and 9.7 percent are living in poverty.

Class distinctions are not clear-cut, but generally, those at the top own lots of land or big businesses or control politics. Middle-class citizens own medium-sized farms or businesses, work for the government, teach, or are professionals such as doctors, dentists, and skilled technicians.

The lower class includes rural workers who own no land, farmers with small plots of land, and blue-collar and unskilled workers such as those who work in factories. The unemployed in both the cities and the countryside are also counted in the lower class.

A downtrodden area of Montevideo serves as housing for poor people.

INTERNET LINKS

https://www.cia.gov/library/publications/the-world-factbook/geos/uy.html

The *CIA World Factbook* provides up-to-date statistics on Uruguay's population.

https://elpais.com/elpais/2017/11/06/inenglish/1509969553_044435.html

This article from *El País* newspaper asks, "Where Did Uruguay's Indigenous Population Go?"

LIFESTYLE

A child dresses like a gaucho for the annual Patria Gaucha festival in Tacuarembo.

7

URUGUAYANS ENJOY A HIGH
standard of Western-style living,
particularly by Latin American
standards. The country is politically stable,
mostly peaceful, and extreme poverty has
almost been eliminated, though poverty
itself remains among disadvantaged
people. Crime is a problem, especially
petty theft in urban areas directed against
tourists and the wealthy.

Most Uruguayans will describe themselves as cultured, generous, and conservative. They do not like to be ridiculed and tend to be cautious—they try never to rush into things. They are humble about themselves and are very family-oriented.

On the negative side, they themselves say they are frequently late. In fact, one humorist noted, "In Uruguay, nothing starts on time because if one is punctual, one is alone."

Uruguayans are also fiercely egalitarian—they prefer to make things equal for everyone. As this has been part of the general governmental design, before and after the dictatorship, it is no surprise that the national character reflects that.

Two passions that unite Uruguayans are soccer and maté, an herbal tea. It is said that "Uruguayan males are born with a diploma in soccer under their arms." This is definitely their national sport. Maté for them is habitual—much like drinking coffee is for many North Americans.

Uruguayan culture is much like that of its larger neighbors, Brazil and particularly Argentina, where Spanish is also the predominant language. The heritage and values of the gaucho are important to Uruguayans. Family ties are of utmost importance to them as well. Education is universal, free, and compulsory; health care is subsidized.

People sip it throughout the day, and Uruguayans can often be seen carrying a thermos of hot water to use in making maté.

One feature of the Uruguayan character that stems from the indigenous past is called the *Garra Charrúa* (GAR-rah char-ROO-ah), or "Charrúan claw" or "talon." This phrase refers to a character trait of persistence, fierceness, and bravery. When Uruguayans engage in sports, soccer in particular, they say they have the Garra Charrúa, recalling Charrúan Indian qualities of courage and fierceness.

RURAL AND URBAN CLASSES

Uruguay is largely urban, as most people live in or near the cities. The lifestyles of rural folks and city dwellers are quite different.

THE RURAL CLASSES Historically, the interior of the country was settled slowly as people moved to the open grasslands to be closer to their cattle, sheep, and horses. Gradually, during the nineteenth century, fences were built to create large ranches, called *estancias*. The soil in the grasslands is

Folk arts and the rural gaucho lifestyle are celebrated at the Patria Gaucha festival.

not rich enough for intensive farming, so these estancias are used to pasture herds of animals. To run a ranch, only a few people are needed to make sure the fences are mended and the animals are healthy. There are a few class divisions among rural people, which results in some differences in lifestyle.

Ranch owners typically do not live full-time on their isolated ranches. Those who own large plots of land—65,000 acres (26,305 hectares) is not uncommon—are quite wealthy and prefer to live in Montevideo where their families have access to the best private schools and all other urban services. Even the important annual agricultural fair is held in Montevideo. Such ranching elites have traditionally supported the Blanco, or National, Party and in general are more conservative than urban elites.

The large estancias are usually divided into sections for different uses— one for cattle, another for sheep, and one more for crops (usually animal feed), and each section is managed by a foreman. The foremen are often related to the ranch owners. Under the foreman is the ranger, who is like a modern gaucho. The rangers, in turn, may supervise a few ranch hands, or helpers, who do the more ordinary tasks, like chores.

Far from the center, life in the countryside is much slower but is also much more hierarchical. Uruguayan egalitarianism apparently doesn't extend as far in this realm. Ranch owners or foremen are unlikely to socialize with their rangers or ranch hands, for example, and they would rarely permit a marriage across these divisions. Being more isolated from trends in the cities has also meant that rural workers tend to be more religious and are less likely to become members of labor unions.

Only those families who can afford to send their children to live in towns can guarantee that the teens will get a high school education. The poorest 5 percent of the population are the ranch hands, who make little money, and the owners of small farms, who cannot afford to travel to the city to take advantage of urban services.

THE URBAN CLASSES Class divisions are also found in the cities. At the top of the heap are the business and political elites. Those are the families that have historically controlled trade and government. The business and industrial elites during the nineteenth century were considered inferior to

People walk along a street in the center of Montevideo.

the landowning class. This changed during the twentieth century, so now the big ranching and business families tend to intermarry and combine their interests. Together, they form the richest 5 percent of the population.

The political elite is composed of a small group of families that have traditionally sent their sons to law school to give them a strong base from which to enter politics. Nowadays, there are more political parties, and control of the government is not restricted to a few important families. There still are "political families," but in fact, the newer parties are being led by middle-class teachers, lawyers, and civil servants—and women, too.

The urban middle class includes professionals, teachers, business managers, and owners of small businesses. They are not quite the majority of the population, but that group is definitely the one setting the standard in Uruguayan society.

As the economy worsened in the 1960s, middle-class women started joining the workforce to supplement their family income. That trend mirrors what happened in North America at the same time. One critical difference is that the middle class in Uruguay can often afford to hire female servants to help around the house, making it easier for Uruguayan women to work outside the home without having to work at home, too.

At the bottom of the income scale are the blue-collar workers and urban poor. Uruguay has never had a very large industrial workforce simply because its small size meant that there were never many industries. Those who do work in industry, however, have tended to maintain a reasonable standard of living with the help of the unions. All urban industries are unionized in Uruguay, and that has meant that workers have been well protected. Like middle-class women, working-class women have had to join the workforce if they can, but since they cannot afford domestic help, they often work twice as hard.

Gaucho traditions and clothing date back to Spanish colonial times. There were no fences to mark property, and cattle and sheep roamed freely. The first Spaniards to take advantage of such herds were a hardy group of expert horsemen who galloped across the plains, rounding up cattle and sheep as they rode. They lived on the land and camped out for days on end, far from the nearest shelter. Their main diet was beef cooked over open fires, washed down with maté. Those early gauchos were tough, independent men who conveyed an image of self-sufficiency that is romanticized today.

Typical gaucho dress developed from the demands of rough outdoor living and long days of horseback riding. Gauchos always carried a large blanket with a hole in the middle that could double as a raincoat, poncho, or sleeping bag. They also wore something called a chiripá (chee-ree-PAH), which was a sort of skirt worn over the seat of the trousers to protect their pants from wear from the saddle. The gauchos' shirts and  *pants were always loose and baggy to permit free movement. They wore* rastras *(RAHS-trahs), or wide belts, made of leather with metal ornamentation—often gold or silver—and soft leather boots. The whole outfit was topped with a soft, brimmed hat of black felt.*

Essential equipment for the gaucho included a horse and saddle, of course, a long knife called a façon *(FAH-sone), and the bola, or boleadora (the projectile weapon of rocks and leather thongs used to bring down big animals).*

In the 1870s wealthy people started buying pieces of land and fencing in the animals. Fences spelled the end of the gaucho era, since those fiercely independent men were forced to work for landowners—to work, moreover, in much more confined areas. Today there are still ranch hands on horseback, but their clothes have been modernized and their open-air way of life is no longer carefree and independent.

Some working-class families have been unable to earn sufficient income in the usual way to survive. Over the last few years, there has been an increase in what is known as informal sector activities. Those are income-generating practices that are not reported to the government, either because people don't want to pay taxes or because they are illegal. Some examples of work in the informal sector are domestic work, trading in goods smuggled in from Brazil, and piecework such as sewing or knitting at home.

Also included in the lowest income group are the unemployed and retired people who live only on government pensions.

FAMILY LIFE AND GENDER ROLES

As in other Latin American countries, family ties are very strong. The ideal family model is both the nuclear and the extended family. A nuclear family is made up of the father and mother and their children. An extended family includes the grandparents, the adult children, and their spouses and children. The extended family is more likely to be found in rural areas, though recently there are more extended families living together in cities. That is because young married couples are finding it more and more difficult to afford their own apartment or house.

In the cities, family size is quite small, the average being two children per couple. As the children grow up, they will live with their parents until they themselves are married. But it is not unusual for people in their thirties to continue to live at home because they are unmarried or cannot afford a place of their own.

COMPADRAZGO   One practice that has continued in the countryside is *compadrazgo* (cohm-pah-DRAHZ-go) or godparenthood. When a baby is baptized, the parents choose two godparents (a man and a woman, not necessarily married to each other) to help the child through various stages of its life. The usual pattern is for the new parents to choose godparents who are richer than they are.

The relationship between godchild and godparents is lifelong—godparents help their godchildren with schooling and finding a job, as well as helping

THE STRUGGLE FOR WOMEN'S RIGHTS

At the beginning of the twentieth century Uruguayan women had very few rights. Their husbands were legally responsible for them and their property. If a woman were given money or land by her father, she lost control of it when she married. She also did not have the right to sue for divorce, although a husband might beat and even kill his wife if he caught her with another man. She could not vote and was treated basically as a child by the legal system. Women did not earn the same amount of money for work of comparable value and were expected to stay home and raise children.

José Batlle's reforms made some progress with divorce laws, but women themselves had to organize and fight for their rights. One outstanding woman who made a difference was Paulina Luisi. She was born in 1875 and became the first Uruguayan woman to get a medical degree. Throughout her life, she was committed to children's welfare and women's rights to education and to the vote. She represented Uruguay at a number of international conferences on women's and children's issues and was the first woman to serve as an official representative of her government at an intergovernmental conference in 1923.

Women demonstrate for gender equality on International Women's Day in Montevideo in 2017.

Along with other feminists, both male and female, Luisi managed to see women get the vote in 1938 for the first time. Finally, in 1946, the Law of Civil Rights of Women was passed, guaranteeing women equality with men. Luisi died in 1949, but she will always be remembered as an inspiration to women everywhere struggling for their rights.

them start families of their own. In return, the godchild will lend a hand to the godparents whenever asked and may even vote the way they vote as a display of loyalty. Those kinds of ties across class and family lines create a network of durable relationships that bind a community together.

WOMEN'S ROLES   Women in Uruguay have had the benefit of legal protection and hard-won rights for much longer than their neighbors. There is still an expectation that men should be "macho"—that they will be the breadwinners and heads of their families. It is quite acceptable for women to work outside the home, but they are still responsible for child care and domestic tasks as well, including shopping, cleaning, and cooking.

Young girls, especially in the cities, are given the same educational opportunities as boys. In the countryside, poor families often cannot afford to send all their children to high school and will choose to educate the boys before girls, believing that their future chances for getting work will be greater. Girls from poorer families often migrate to towns or big cities to find work as live-in domestic servants.

In 2014, President José Mujica signed a new law that legalized abortion in the first twelve weeks of pregnancy (fourteen weeks in cases of rape). Uruguay thus became the first country in South America to decriminalize abortion. Most Latin American nations ban the procedure outright. Prior to its legalization in Uruguay, some 30 percent of maternal deaths in that country were due to unsafe, clandestine abortions. Among low-income women, the percentage was nearly half.

EDUCATION

Uruguay was the first country in Latin America to have free, universal, and compulsory education. In 1877 the Law of Common Education was passed, making education available to all school-age children. Uruguay also has one of the best school systems and literacy rates in Latin America. Literacy is estimated at 98 percent, and there is no difference between men and women in this regard. Also, nearly 100 percent of school-age children attend

elementary school. The first nine years of school are compulsory; children are required to attend school until they are fourteen years old.

Schoolchildren in public schools do not have to wear uniforms, but they must wear smocks over their clothes. That depicts all children as equal, whether rich or poor. Public schools are free and secular. There are also private schools in the cities that cater to wealthy families. Two classes of Uruguayans rarely go to university: the urban poor, who must start working young to supplement the family income; and rural families who cannot afford the living expenses of students away from home.

There is one public university and five private universities in Montevideo. The University of the Republic is publicly supported and free to anyone who has completed high school, although students do have to pay for books, and there are some small fees for the use of university facilities. Private universities such as the Catholic University charge tuition fees.

The average university program takes four to six years, but most students take longer to finish. There are discounts on public transportation

A teacher in a rural school helps a student use a laptop computer. The Uruguayan government provided free laptops to all school children in 2007.

for undergraduates and subsidized cafeterias with inexpensive food for all students. With a scarcity of jobs for graduates, there is little incentive to graduate quickly.

HEALTH

Health care, along with other social programs, is subsidized by the government. Subsidized care is not universal, however; those who can afford private health care are expected to pay for it. Uruguayans have adequate facilities nationwide for medical care.

In 2017, the average life expectancy at birth in Uruguay was 74.2 years for men and 80.6 years for women, for an average of 77.4 years. Those numbers were improvements over those from ten years before, and place Uruguay at number 70 in the world for life expectancy, which is not a great score, but is one of the highest in South America. (For comparison, the average life expectancy in 2017 was 80 years in the United States.)

HOUSING

In the cities there are both apartment buildings and single family houses. On the outskirts are areas of suburban family homes. In the bigger cities, there is also public housing, which is subsidized by the government for low-income tenants.

In the countryside, being rich or poor makes a huge difference in how one lives. The poorest agricultural workers subsist in shantytowns of shoddily constructed shacks that do not have running water or sewage systems. By contrast, the rich live in sprawling ranch houses that were often built in the nineteenth century and modernized over time. They are normally big, one-storied buildings. The walls are solidly constructed, and the rooms are large enough to entertain many guests. Ranches are usually separated by great distances, so when ranch owners and their families visited one another, they would often stay for days. For that reason, houses were built with extra bedrooms and big dining and living rooms. Today some of those homes are open to tourists who want to see what life is like out in the open grasslands.

MANNER OF DRESS

There is no national dress or manner of dressing that distinguishes Uruguayans from any other modern Western people. About the only thing that sets apart urban Latin Americans from urban North Americans is that their dress codes are slightly more formal in the south. Latin American women also tend to dress more often in skirts than in pants.

The only traditional dress one finds in Uruguay comes from the gauchos. The gaucho, or cowboy, heritage of Uruguay is very important and people work hard at preserving it. The gaucho image still symbolizes a glorious past of freedom and self-reliance for modern Uruguayans. Gaucho traditions are celebrated during a special festival once a year.

INTERNET LINKS

https://www.nytimes.com/2016/06/28/opinion/from-uruguay-a -model-for-making-abortion-safer.html
This article examines the circumstances surrounding the legalization of abortion in Uruguay.

http://www.oecd.org/education/school/OECD%20Reviews%20of%20 School%20Resources_Uruguay_Summary_EN.pdf
This 2016 report takes a look at the strengths and weaknesses of Uruguay's education system.

https://www.tripsavvy.com/gauchos-of-argentina-uruguay -southern-brazil-1636613
A story about the gauchos of yesteryear and today.

http://www.who.int/gho/countries/ury.pdf?ua=1
The World Health Organization provides a statistical profile of health in Uruguay.

RELIGION

The Church of Iglesia de Maria Auxiliadora in Mercedes, Uruguay, gleams against a bright blue sky.

THE ROMAN CATHOLIC CHURCH played an enormous role in the European settlement of Latin America. In many Central American, South American, and Caribbean countries, it still does today. But not in Uruguay. According to a 2013 poll conducted by the Pew Research Center, some 37 percent of Uruguayans claimed to be atheist or agnostic or to have no particular religion. These statistics include some overlap, as some people identify themselves as Catholic by upbringing but nonreligious in practice.

A SECULAR SOCIETY

Compared with most of its neighbors in South America, Uruguay has been much less influenced by the Roman Catholic Church from colonial times to the present. Historically, Spain sent out conquistadores and priests together to take over native societies and convert them to Catholicism. However, the presence of priests in Uruguay was always relatively small.

8

Uruguay is by far Latin America's most secular country, with the separation of church and state being deeply embedded in its culture. It is tolerant of other faiths, and the right to religious freedom is spelled out in its constitution.

The Basilica of the Holy Sacrament in Colonia del Sacramento is the oldest church in the country.

When Uruguay became independent and the first constitution was written, Catholicism was the official religion, but the constitution protected the people's right to religious freedom. As early as 1844, British traders living in Montevideo were allowed to build an Anglican church for themselves. That was one of the first Protestant churches in Spanish America. In 1935, when the English church was in the way of a new sea wall planned for the city, the government paid to have it moved stone by stone to another site, because it was considered a historical landmark.

Since independence, Uruguay has become more and more secularized and fewer events depend on church participation. For example, in 1837 civil marriages were made legal. In 1861 the state nationalized public cemeteries so that the Catholic Church could not prevent non-Catholics from being buried in them.

During José Batlle's two terms as president (1903—1907 and 1911—1915), many more secular laws were enacted. Batlle believed that all religions should be tolerated equally and that none should control people's lives in a legal way. In 1907 he made divorce legal. In Catholicism, divorce is prohibited, and if two people want to end their marriage, they must get special permission from the Church. Many Catholics believe it is a sin to divorce. With its new law, the state gave permission to divorce to couples who wanted to end their marriage.

In 1909 all religious instruction was banned from public schools. The constitution created by Batlle and finally passed in 1919 officially separated church and state, and Catholicism was no longer the recognized religion of Uruguay. According to the principle of separation of church and state, references to God were removed from the parliamentary oath and religious references were dropped from the names of cities and villages.

ROMAN CATHOLICS

Even among the remaining Catholics in Uruguay, the church may play a minimal role in their lives. According to the *CIA World Factbook*, in 2006, about 47.1 percent of the Uruguayan population identified themselves as Catholic. Most Catholic babies are still baptized, but in the capital only about 10 percent of Catholics attend mass on Sundays. Generally, church attendance is higher in rural areas than in the cities and is higher among women than among men.

Protestants make up 11.1 percent of the population, nondenominational Christians make up 23.2 percent, 0.3 percent are Jewish, and 18.3 percent do not adhere to any particular religion or believe in other faiths.

The Church of Our Lady of Candelaria in Punta del Este is popular with tourists.

In many South American societies, folk beliefs have arisen from indigenous cultures. The new settlers taught their religion to the natives and in exchange learned about their beliefs and superstitions. With such a small original indigenous population, Uruguayans did not have much opportunity to learn from those original inhabitants. So such folk tradition that does exist in Uruguay comes largely from the time when many Uruguayan men were gauchos roughing it in the open plains.

One folk belief inspired from this gaucho era is that one should never kill fireflies. These flickering insects are thought to keep the spirits of the dead company at night with their little lamps. Another rural superstition, which grew out of the indigenous Guarani mythology, is that a son born seventh in line will periodically turn into an animal such as a wolf, pig, or goat. He is called Lobizón (oh-bee-SON), from lobo, or "wolf." This is similar to the European werewolf superstition that the full moon makes those who have been bitten by a wolf turn into a mutant creature, half-man and half-wolf.

OTHER RELIGIONS

PROTESTANTS   There have been Protestants in Uruguay since at least 1844 when the first Anglican church was built. During the twentieth century, many other Protestant churches were established in Uruguay, part of the larger trend of Protestantization in Catholic South America. Many American evangelical churches set up in Uruguay since the 1960s, and have been hard at work to convert Catholics to Protestantism. Since Uruguayans are not very religious to start with, the new missionaries have managed to attract only small congregations.

Some of the Protestant churches represented in Uruguay include Baptists, Seventh-day Adventists, Methodists, and the Evangelical Mennonite Church. Altogether, they account for approximately 11.1 percent of the population.

UMBANDA   A syncretic religion that largely developed in the early 1900s in Brazil, Umbanda also has followers in Uruguay. It is a fusion of African traditions with Roman Catholicism, Spiritism, and Indigenous American beliefs. Among its distinctive practices is the intercession of psychic priests or priestesses with spirits of the dead on behalf of the living. They also revere the Catholic saints. The number of faithful is difficult to determine because many Umbanda followers call themselves Catholics, though the Catholic Church itself rejects that notion.

JEWS Before the repression and dictatorship there was a sizable Jewish community in Montevideo. There were six active synagogues with large congregations. Today only 0.3 percent of the total population are Jews.

Jews had migrated to Uruguay because it was known to have a religiously tolerant society. The first large wave of European Jewish immigrants came at the beginning of the twentieth century. The second wave of mostly German Jews arrived in the 1930s when the Nazis were beginning to persecute the Jews in Germany. Many Uruguayan Jews left Uruguay during the repression in the 1970s, so now they are only a tiny fraction of the society.

INTERNET LINKS

http://www.pewforum.org/2014/11/13/religion-in-latin-america
This report gives an in-depth look at religion in Latin America, and includes significant references to Uruguay.

http://www.religionfacts.com/umbanda
A quick overview of Umbanda is provided on this site.

LANGUAGE

A little girl practices her handwriting in a village school in Jaureguiberry.

9

LANGUAGE REFLECTS THE HISTORY OF a people and country, and in Uruguay, that language is Spanish—the tongue of the first Europeans to explore and settle the land. Uruguayans today speak Spanish, but the language has various peculiarities that make it a bit different. Some Uruguayans speak various colorful dialects that were created through a blending of other languages.

SPANISH IN THE NEW WORLD

The language spoken in Uruguay and most of the rest of South America is Spanish, with the notable exception of Brazil, where Portuguese is spoken. That fact is taken for granted today because it is well known that the first foreign settlers of the continent were from Spain.

Many languages were spoken in Spain way back when settlers were first arriving in South America. To list some examples, in the fifteenth and sixteenth centuries such languages as Castilian, Catalan, Asturian, Leonese, Aragonese, Basque, and Galician were all spoken in different regions of the country. Castilian, Catalan, Galician, and Basque are four that have survived into the twenty-first century and can be heard spoken today.

A welcome sign in the container port district of Montevideo includes several languages.

Why did a particular language spoken in only some parts of Spain become the single dominant language in all of Spain's New World colonies? The answer is that migration to the New World followed a specific pattern.

All settlement in the New World from Spain was planned in the province of Castile in central Spain, so that those applying for consent to leave Spain had to have learned enough Castilian to make an application. Those chosen were sent to either Andalusia or Seville to wait for a boat to take them across the Atlantic Ocean. The waiting often took as much as a year, during which time the emigrants learned the local language.

In addition, ships' crews were all from Andalusia or the Canary Islands, which had become a province of Spain in the late 1400s. Since crossing the ocean took such a long time, ships had to stop in the Canary Islands to reprovision. All New World settlers followed that route, so most of them came to speak a common language by the time they arrived in their new homes. The fact that Castilian and Andalusian are quite similar reinforced the trend toward a common language. At the same time, Castilian Spanish became increasingly more common throughout all of Spain because it was the language of the king and his court. So after five centuries, people in Latin America and in Spain both speak a language that is quite similar but not exactly the same.

The Spanish spoken in Latin America has been influenced by such other agents as time and distance. Those factors led to differences in pronunciation and word usage. Hence, the Spanish of the New World settled by the Spanish is not exactly the same as the language that came to dominate modern Spain.

Some of the differences in vocabularies between modern Spain and Latin America can be traced to the time the settlers spent in port towns or on board ships. Many words that are used every day in Latin America are used only on board ships in Spain.

Other words in Latin American Spanish are from a very old form of the language and are no longer used at all in European Spanish. Some examples of those are *lindo* (beautiful), *cobija* (blanket), and *pollera* (skirt).

Latin America	Spain	English Translation
botar	*tirar*	to throw out
amarrar	*atar*	to tie up
balde	*cubo*	bucket
timón	*volante*	steering wheel

INFLUENCE OF THE INDIGENOUS PEOPLES

Although most of the original populations were killed off early in Uruguay's history, there are some remnants of their languages on the map of Uruguay. Río Yi was named by the Charrúas—the tribe that was traitorously massacred—who also used the boleadora, or bola, the weapon of leather thongs and rocks used to entangle animals. This was adopted by the gauchos and is still called by its Charrúan name.

Place names such as Paysandú and Yaguarí come from the language of the Guaraní. Since those populations—the Charrúas and the Guaraní—were

Spanish is said to be one of the easiest languages for English speakers to learn. Unlike in English, letters consistently make the same sounds, so essentially, what is read is what is said. The Spanish alphabet, shown here, has extra consonants.

a b c ch d e f g h i j k l ll m n ñ o p q r s t u v w x y z

There are five main vowel sounds:

  a = *ah*= *like the a in cat, so* alma *(soul) is AHL-mah*

  e = *ay*= *like the ay in day, so* mente *(mind) is MAYN-tay*

  i = *ee* = *like the ee in teeth, so* infinitud *(infinity) is een-feen-ee-TOOD*

  o = *oh*= *like the o in bone, so* poco *(little) is POH-koh*

  u = *oo*= *like the sound in chew or zoo, so* una *(a) is OO-nah*

Sometimes there are combinations of vowels, for example ia or ue. Each vowel is pronounced separately. So ia becomes ee-ah and ue becomes oo-ay.

Most Spanish consonants are the same as English ones, but there are a few differences:

  ch = *same as the English sound in church, so* che *(a term of address) is chay*

  ll = *same sound as l + y in English, so* calle *("street") is cahl-ye*

  ñ = *same sound as n + y in English, so* mañana *("morning," "tomorrow") is pronounced man-yan-ah*

  h = *always silent, so* hambre *("hunger") is AM-bray*

  j = *like the English h in hat, so* pájaro *("bird") is PAH-ha-row*

  qu = *like the English k in keep, so* pequeño *("small") is pay-KAYN-yo*

  v = *like the English b, but a little softer*

  x = *like the English s except when it is between two vowels, then it is an h sound, so* oxicanto *is oh-hee-CAN-toh*

  y = *like the English sh, as in mission*

  z = *like the English s in so, so* azul *("blue") is AH-sool*

The letters c and g are tricky because they each have two pronunciations:

  c with e or i has an s sound, so lúcida *("lucid" or "clear") is LOO-see-dah; but c with a, o, or u is hard, like k, so* buscar *("to look for") is BOOS-kar*

  g with e or i has an h sound, but g with a, o, or u is hard, like the English g in gut, so frágil *("fragile") is FRAH-heel, but* siga *("I follow") is SEE-gah*

very small and did not mix for long with Spanish speakers, there are no obvious influences on Uruguayan Spanish other than these few words.

THE SPANISH OF URUGUAY

The official language of Uruguay is Spanish, but the reality of what people speak in daily life and why they speak that way is more complex. In Uruguay, as in any other country, there are historical influences from other languages and other times.

Most of the immigrants from Spain came from Castile, Andalusia, Galicia, and the Canary Islands, and they all took the peculiarities of their local Spanish with them. An example is the Canary usage of *pibe/piba* for guy/gal. These words are not commonly heard outside Uruguay and Argentina.

For a period in the eighteenth and nineteenth centuries, Montevideo was the main port for the trade in African slaves. Some words from African languages are still used. *Mucama* means a female domestic servant, and *candombe* (can-DOME-bey) is an African-based carnival ritual and dance.

There were also a significant number of Italian immigrants to the Río de la Plata area in the first half of the twentieth century. They used their own language for a while before becoming fluent in Spanish. One of the words that has entered Uruguayan Spanish from Italian is *chau* (*ciao* in Italian), which means "good-bye."

DIALECTS

Uruguay's location between Argentina and Brazil, and the fact that it was a province of Brazil briefly in the nineteenth century, explains the Portuguese influence in Uruguayan Spanish. There is even a whole separate language that combines Spanish and Portuguese and is spoken only along the Brazil-Uruguay border.

An old travel poster from the 1930s shows a bathing beauty on the beach.

COCOLICHE AND GAUCHO SPEECH

Cocoliche was a version of Spanish spoken by Italian immigrants in the early part of the twentieth century. When the first Italian immigrants were trying to learn Spanish, they found it easier at first to combine the language of their new country with their native tongue, mixing vocabulary and grammatical forms to create a very distinctive dialect. The second generation grew up learning fluent Spanish in the schools, and Cocoliche faded away.

Gaucho speech, a rural variety of language, preserves older words and forms of grammar. To a Spanish-speaking person, gaucho speech today might sound something like Shakespearean English to an American. Gaucho speech is associated with the lifestyle of those legendary men who roamed the open grasslands, herding wild cattle and horses. The idiom is preserved in early poetry and novels, but today, a real gaucho is very rare and so, too, is his particular variety of Spanish.

Although Uruguay is not a big or populous country compared with its neighbors, it is big enough to have regional variations in language. The majority of the population lives in Montevideo where the dialect is virtually the same as that in Buenos Aires, Argentina. This dialect is called Porteño (por-TAYN-yoh) and is very distinctive. Part of the vocabulary of Porteño comes from a working-class slang called Lunfardo (loon-FAR-doh). The special words used by poorer people came to be used by the population as a whole through the lyrics of popular music, especially the pervasive tango music.

In the interior of the country, people speak a couple of different dialects. The most notable is Fronterizo (fron-tayr-EE-zoh), which is spoken close to the Brazilian frontier in the north. Fronterizo (also called Portuñol and Bayano) combines features of Spanish and Portuguese and is considered to be a third language. Uruguayans have learned this language because for some time there have been better educational facilities and employment opportunities in Brazil than in Uruguay. The populations living along the border have socialized and lived together for many years; this fusion language is the result.

Two types of speech that have passed out of use are Cocoliche (ko-ko-LEE-chay) and the gaucho language. Those once vibrant dialects were spoken by particular groups in Uruguayan society. Because those groups no longer exist, the languages they spoke have also disappeared from daily life, but they have an afterlife in poetry and the theater.

INTERNET LINKS

https://alphaomegatranslations.com/foreign-language/speaking-the-spanish-of-uruguay
This site provides an overview of Spanish language in Uruguay.

http://www.omniglot.com/language/articles/latin_american_spanish.htm
This site looks at the variations of Spanish spoken in Latin America, including in Uruguaya.

https://www.omniglot.com/writing/spanish.htm
Omniglot provides an introduction to the Spanish language.

https://www.worldatlas.com/articles/languages-of-uruguay.html
A quick discussion of the languages of Uruguay is covered on this page.

ARTS

An artist sells his paintings depicting local scenes to tourists along the Montevideo waterfront.

10

FROM THE STREET ART OF THE barrios to the prominent works displayed in the National Museum of Visual Arts in Montevideo, Uruguay has a rich arts culture. With a historically high level of education and popular support for the arts, many types of creative expression have flourished in the small republic.

Uruguay has produced world-renowned painters, writers, and composers. Theatergoing is a popular activity, presenting works ranging from locally produced plays to Shakespeare. Music and dance is vitally important, especially the tango and candombe.

Candombe drummers perform during Carnival festivities in the capital city.

PERFORMING ARTS

Performing arts include music, theater, and dance. As a largely urban people, Uruguayans have a splendid and varied tradition of performing arts. Most of this vitality is centered in Montevideo, but department capitals and larger towns often support local theaters and performing musicians.

THEATER The Teatro Solís (Solís Theater) in Montevideo is the home of the National Comedy Repertory Company. This group of actors and directors regularly performs new and classic works by Latin American playwrights.

The most famous of Uruguayan playwrights is Florencio Sánchez (1875– 1910), who wrote plays set in the Río de la Plata region. His characters are usually Uruguayan, Argentinian, or Paraguayan and tend to represent the working class. His plays are famous for their realistic dialogue and insightful portrayal of life in the slums of Buenos Aires or Montevideo. Some of his plays examine the conflicts arising between rural lifestyles and the modern changes introduced by the cities. Sánchez has been compared with famous

The Teatro Solís is the country's oldest theater.

Russian authors such as Dostoevsky and Gorky, who dealt with social confrontations.

Past literary figures such as Pedro Figari, José Enrique Rodó, and Mario Benedetti were internationally acclaimed. A notable modern playwright is Mauricio Rosencof (b. 1933). He began writing in the 1960s but then decided to join the Tupamaros in their fight against the government. He was arrested and jailed for more than ten years. Whenever he was allowed to have paper, he continued to write poetry in jail, mostly about what it feels like to be tortured and imprisoned. He was released in 1985 along with other Tupamaros.

Other theaters in Montevideo include the Odeón, which features productions of Shakespeare's plays along with modern dramas, and the Verdi, which produces mostly comedies. Universities and many secondary schools around the country support amateur theater groups. Uruguay also has a highly regarded independent theater movement that served as an outlet through which Uruguayans were able to express themselves politically, especially during the 1960s.

A couple dances in public in Montevideo on International Tango Day, December 11.

DANCE AND MUSIC Perhaps the best-known music from this part of the world is the tango. The tango is most often associated with Buenos Aires, but Buenos Aires and Montevideo are culturally almost indistinguishable, and the dance began in the poorer neighborhoods of the cities in the 1880s.

The tango is both a type of dance and a special kind of music. A standard tango band has to include six players: two *bandoneons* (ban-doh-NAY-ons, a type of accordion made in Germany), two violins, a piano, and a double bass. At first the tango was only music and a style of intimate dance for men and women. Then in the early 1900s, the lyrics became just as important as the music and the dance. The lyrics tended to have sad themes such as break-ups between lovers and street-life issues of the poor. Tango clubs opened all over

Since the early days of independence, songwriters have told stories about the civil wars between the Colorados and the Blancos and have poked fun at their enemies in their songs. In more recent times, three performing art forms featuring songs have become the favored media for political observation: Carnival murgas *(MOOR-gahs), the tango, and the* canto popular *(KAHN-toh poh-poo-LAHR).*

Murgas are written to be sung as part of street theater productions that take place in every neighborhood during Carnival (Mardi Gras). Those catchy songs frequently focus on some politician or political event from the past year. Murgas also refers to the bands that perform them.

Tango songs are usually about the conflicts between men and women, especially of the lower classes. While singing about relationships, they also describe the life of the urban poor and new immigrants. In that sense, the tango becomes social commentary about life on the seedy streets.

Canto popular (popular song) started in the late 1960s when young musicians all over Latin America began to write songs about social problems and politics. They criticized their countries' governments and wanted to see changes in their countries. In Uruguay, canto popular was heavily censored by the military, and many musicians were arrested or forced to leave the country. Some continued to try to make their messages heard through informal concerts and underground recordings. They were saluted as the only voice of the people under the systems of repression imposed by the army and police.

Montevideo and Buenos Aires, and artists made a living by selling records and giving live performances. The most famous tango ever, "La Cumparsita," was written by a Uruguayan artist, Gerardo H. Matos Rodríguez (1897—1948).

Another popular art form is the candombe, which originated in the African-Uruguayan community. Candombe refers to both the music and the dance. The music is distinctive as it uses special African drums called *tamboriles* (tahm-BOR-eel-ehs). Candombe music and dance are part of two festivals celebrated in Montevideo.

Both the tango and candombe have been recognized by UNESCO as examples of the Intangible Cultural Heritage of Humanity.

Uruguay has produced two classical composers: Eduardo Fabini (1882—

1950) and Héctor Errecart (1923–2002). Fabini is famous for his symphonies, while Errecart adapted traditional gaucho music to a classical form. His use of folk music themes earned him world renown.

VISUAL ARTS

Uruguay has a long tradition of supporting the visual arts and has produced some important artists. One of the most famous is the post-impressionist painter Pedro Figari (1861–1938), who gained international recognition for his works.

Another artist who tried to capture rural living in his work is the printmaker Carlos González (1905–1993). His woodblock prints portray old-fashioned country life and focuses especially on gaucho culture. Many of his woodcuts depict gauchos in typical scenes: huddled over a campfire for warmth at night or sharing some maté on the plains. González's style is called primitivism because he uses very simple lines and carves only with a knife, making his work appear a little rough, much like his subjects.

José Belloni's bronze monument of a pioneer wagon dates to 1934.

The nineteenth-century Realist painter Juan Manuel Blanes (1830–1901) is one of Uruguay's most celebrated artists. He is well-known for his paintings of historical events, such as the painting *Oath of the Thirty-Three Easterners* (1878). It hangs today in the Juan Manuel Blanes Municipal Museum of the Arts in Montevideo.

Another prominent artist was Joaquín Torres García (1874–1949), who was very active in the modern art community in Europe.

In Montevideo's parks, examples of Uruguayan sculpture can be seen. Perhaps the most photographed of all is the sculpture of the covered wagon or *carreta* (car-RAY-tah) being pulled by six oxen and driven by a bearded man. That well-known work represents the pioneers who first left the shores of the Río de la Plata to settle the interior of the country. The sculpture is by José Belloni (1882–1965) and stands in Batlle and Ordoñez Park.

A portrait of writer José Enrique Rodo graces an older 200 peso note.

Another very famous sculpture is the gaucho on his horse that stands at the intersection of two large streets in downtown Montevideo. That much-photographed piece was made by José Luis Zorrilla de San Martín (1891—1975), son of a famous writer.

LITERARY ARTS

Literature is the area of artistic endeavor in which Uruguay has most excelled. As a result of a high literacy rate and a commitment to freedom of speech, Uruguayans have turned more often to writing to express themselves than to any other art form. Many early works focused on nationalistic themes and on the rural heritage of the country.

Juan Zorrilla de San Martín (1855—1931), father of sculptor José Luis, was both a poet and a diplomat. In 1879 he wrote the poem "La leyenda pátria" ("The Patriotic Legend") in tribute to Uruguay's history. His other famous poem is the epic Tabaré, a long adventure story about Charrúa Indians. It is read throughout southern Latin America. Zorilla also started a public newspaper in 1878 and served as Uruguay's ambassador to the Vatican, France, and Spain.

Javier de Viana (1868—1926) wrote about the end of the gaucho era. He captured the poverty and tragedy of gaucho life in his novel Gaucha. Eduardo Acevedo Díaz (1851—1921) also portrayed gaucho life in his book Soledad (Solitude), published in 1894, but with a more upbeat tone.

Probably the most influential book ever written by an Uruguayan is Ariel by José Enrique Rodó (1872—1917). Written in 1900 when Rodó was only twenty-nine, the book is actually a speech given by a fictitious teacher to his students. The students call the teacher Prospero because he keeps a big statue of Ariel in his study.

Prospero and Ariel are characters from William Shakespeare's play The Tempest. In The Tempest, the main character is a magician, Prospero, who lives alone on an island with his daughter and a savage, Caliban. Prospero's magic comes from a beautiful spirit he controls named Ariel. Ariel represents

JUANA DE AMERICA

Juana de Ibarbourou is one of Uruguay's best-loved poets. She was born in Melo in 1892 and started publishing her poetry in 1918 when she moved to Montevideo. In her early life, she wrote and published plentifully and became very popular both within and outside of Uruguay. In 1929 she was nicknamed Juana de America ("Juana of America") in a public ceremony in her honor at the University of the Republic.

Throughout her life, she faced many tragedies, including the deaths of her parents and of her husband. Those events are reflected in her poetry, which is sometimes very sad and religious.

In 1947 she was elected to the Academy of Fine Arts. In 1957 she was honored by UNESCO in a special meeting in her honor. Her works have all been reprinted many times and some have been translated into English. She died poor and nearly forgotten in Montevideo in 1979, but the public remembered her contributions to Uruguayan art, and she was given a state funeral complete with the national flag on her coffin.

light and virtue, whereas Caliban represents greed and elemental impulses. Shakespeare's play serves as the framework used by the lecturing teacher to admonish his students how they should live their lives. He tells them they should try to develop all their human qualities, not just the ones that satisfy basic needs such as hunger and thirst. In other words, they should try to be more like Ariel than Caliban.

Rodó's book suggested that the US model of development was materialistic, like Caliban, whereas Latin American development should be idealistic, like Ariel. This was one of the most significant early efforts by Latin American thinkers to define the differences between South American and North American values.

EDUARDO GALEANO

Eduardo Hughes Galeano was born in Montevideo in 1940. He started writing for a literary journal called Marcha, *which was well-known for its high quality of writing. During the repression of the 1970s, the military shut down Marcha and imprisoned Galeano. He eventually fled the country. He returned in 1984 to become the editor of a new journal,* Brecha.

His most famous book is Open Veins of Latin America, *a history of Latin America from the European conquest to 1971 (when the book was first published). It is a political commentary on how the people of Latin America have been used first by the Spanish and Portuguese and then by other more powerful nations. At the time, the book was banned in Uruguay, Argentina, and Chile. It has since been issued in over thirty editions and remains on reading lists in universities around the world.*

His Memory of Fire, *published in 1988, is a collection of stories, poems, newspaper articles, and reports detailing life in Latin America from before the European conquest to the present. It complements* Open Veins, *which is more of a straightforward history.*

Galeano has also written fiction. His most notable novel, Days and Nights of Love and War, *is about living in a military dictatorship, based on experiences in a repressive Uruguay. Galeano was also a devoted soccer fan, and in 1995, wrote* Football (Soccer) in Sun and Shadow, *which has been hailed as one of the greatest books ever written about the sport. The prolific author died in 2015 in Montevideo from lung cancer at age seventy-four.*

FOLK CULTURE

Folk culture or folk art refers to the culture and art of the common people. Into this category falls much of the people's art of rural Uruguay. One particularly special type of folk craft is the maté cup and straw. Traditionally, people drank maté from a hollowed-out gourd that was often decorated with silver. To drink out of the gourd, they used a silver straw called a *bombilla* (bohm-BEE-ya). The set was usually carved in beautiful patterns, and it would have been among the prized possessions of any Uruguayan well off enough to afford it. Nowadays, those items have mostly been replaced with cheaper cups and straws, but older examples can be seen proudly displayed in many homes.

A more modern form of craft is the hand-knit sweater. Those bright and colorful garments are made by women working in their homes. They are thick and warm, and each one is unique. Knitting is an important source of income for poorer women in the countryside and the cities alike.

INTERNET LINKS

https://ich.unesco.org/en/RL/candombe-and-its-socio-cultural-space-a-community-practice-00182
The UNESCO site presents candombe as an example of the intangible cultural heritage of humanity.

https://ich.unesco.org/en/RL/tango-00258
This is the Intangible Cultural Heritage entry for Tango.

http://www.teatrosolis.org.uy/categoria_146_1.html
This is the official site of the Teatro Solis in Montevideo.

https://theculturetrip.com/south-america/uruguay/art
This travel site has links to numerous articles about the arts in Uruguay.

LEISURE

Bathers enjoy the beach in Piriapolis under a beautiful

11

RECREATION IS AN IMPORTANT PART of the Uruguayan lifestyle, and most people have the time and money to enjoy some downtime. Whether playing team sports themselves or just cheering on their favorite teams, many folks are devoted *fútbol* or rugby fans. There are also plenty of other activities for Uruguayans to enjoy in their leisure time.

Uruguayans enjoy a wide variety of indoor and outdoor leisure activities. They also have a deep-seated passion for playing and watching soccer. In the summer, many people take to the water to windsurf or swim. Uruguayans also enjoy going to the movies and cafés, or shopping. They also like to take short vacations.

La Mano (The hand), a gigantic sculpture, is planted on Brava Beach in Punta del Este.

SPORTS

SOCCER The most popular sport in the country is soccer, called fútbol in South America. Every able-bodied boy in Uruguay has played soccer at school or in local fields, and everyone follows his favorite team. On July 13, 1930, the first World Cup soccer finals were held in Montevideo's Centenary Stadium, and Uruguay was one of the competing national teams. Uruguay won the championship, and the celebrations that resulted from that World Cup win are remembered still as the loudest and wildest in the history of the country.

In 1950 the Uruguay national team executed a major upset against heavyweight Brazil, which was favored to win the World Cup that year. The 2—1 victory over Brazil eventually became known as the Maracanzo, or the Maracaná Blow, as the match was played at the Maracaná stadium in Rio de Janeiro in Brazil.

Children play fútbol in a park in Montevideo.

OTHER SPORTS AND COMPETITIONS With so many good beaches lining the Río de la Plata between Montevideo and Punta del Este, water sports are very popular in Uruguay. There are many boat races, both for motorboats and sailboats. Uruguay was once a stopover on one of the world's most prestigious races, the Volvo Ocean Race (formerly known as the Whitbread Round the World Race). During the summer, windsurfing competitions attract international competitors. Swimming is very popular, both as a competitive sport and as recreation. Every year there is a swimming race in the Punta del Este area, east of Montevideo.

Another race that attracts local and international attention is the annual Grand Prix auto race, also in Punta del Este. For people with more pedestrian interests, there is the San Fernando Marathon for runners. Besides water

MIRACLE OF THE ANDES

On October 13, 1972, a chartered Uruguayan airplane slammed into a remote area of the Andes Mountains in Argentina. Onboard were forty-five people, including a Uruguayan rugby team—young men ages nineteen to thirty-three—their friends, and families. They were on their way to a weekend game in Santiago, Chile. Twelve of the passengers died from the crash, and six others succumbed within hours or a few days.

The remaining twenty-seven survivors faced an unimaginable ordeal hampered by altitude sickness, dehydration, snow blindness, malnourishment, and extreme cold. One by one, people died from injuries or starvation. The team members heard from their radio reception that the rescue parties had given up the search for them. In life-or-death desperation, they reluctantly resorted to eating the flesh of the dead in order to survive.

The gruesome ordeal lasted seventy-two days, and only came to an end after two of the men hiked through the mountains to find help. In the end, only sixteen people survived, six of them rugby players.

The true story inspired many books and the movie Alive, *based on a book by Piers Paul Read and starring Ethan Hawke.* National Geographic *also published an article about a team that re-created the brutally hard trek to find help by two of the young men to show what a tough journey it would have been even for trained people with proper equipment.*

The crash site.

In 2007 a documentary film entitled Stranded: I've Come From a Plane That Crashed on the Mountains, *directed by Uruguayan Gonzalo Arijon, recounts one of the best-known twentieth century tales of resilience and survival. After so many years, the survivors who were once labeled cannibals by their own countrymen, finally agreed to talk on camera with startling details, telling what their thoughts about it are today. In 2016, survivor Roberto Canessa, now a prominent pediatric cardiologist in Uruguay, wrote the book,* I Had to Survive.

Cyclists push hard in the last stage of the 2018 Vuelta Ciclista del Uruguay.

sports, Uruguayans enjoy basketball, tennis, polo, and golf. There are also competitions to show purebred Arabian horses, magnificent animals that are the pride of Uruguay.

CYCLING A popular leisure activity in Uruguay is cycling. There are numerous cycling clubs in Uruguay that compete both nationally and internationally. The governing body over cycling races in Uruguay is the Uruguayan Cycling Federation that successfully organized the Road and Track Pan-American Championships in Montevideo in 2008. The country's major cycling competition is the Tour de Uruguay. Many visitors to Uruguay opt to tour the nation on bicycles, rewarding them with intimate glimpses of the land and countrymen of the gauchos.

LEISURE ACTIVITIES

MOVIES AND THEATER One of the most popular forms of entertainment is the cinema. There are movie theaters all over the country. A small local film industry and foreign films provide entertainment variety. In larger urban centers, there is often a lively theater scene. Montevideo attracts international touring shows.

NIGHTLIFE Nightlife includes visiting *peñas* (PAYN-yahs), or clubs with live music. While the peñas tend to be most popular with the young, older people are more likely to go to old-fashioned tango bars to hear live music. For those with a sense of adventure, there are also clubs specializing in candombe, or African-Uruguayan music. Other musical tastes are served by symphony concerts and the occasional opera in Montevideo.

For people on limited budgets, nightlife might include a stroll around the downtown area and a stop in one of Montevideo's many cafés and late-night restaurants. Other types of recreation include gambling at one of the two government-owned casinos in Montevideo, Casino del Parque Rodó and the Hotel Carrasco Casino.

The historic, recently renovated Hotel Casino Carrasco in the Carrasco district of Montevideo is a national landmark.

Independence Square is a popular site in the center of the capital city.

STROLLING Part of the Spanish heritage in Uruguayan culture is a love of strolling. It may not sound like much in the way of entertainment, but there is a long-standing tradition of going for walks with family and friends. In addition to shopping districts, Montevideo has many public parks and gardens well suited to this purpose. A place popular with young people is the Rambla, a road that runs parallel to Montevideo's waterfront. Ideally, a leisurely stroll leads to a coffee, ice cream, or maté with friends.

SHOPPING Window shopping is also very popular. The main shopping street in Montevideo is Eighteenth of July Avenue, which includes classy boutiques from all over the world. Recently, Montevideo has also promoted North American-style shopping malls, and several have sprung up in the city. Two are architecturally quite distinctive: Punta Carretas, a renovated prison, and Barrio Reus, located in a formerly impoverished area of the city. Architectural students renovated that dingy area by painting all the old tenement buildings in bright colors, turning it into a tourist attraction today.

On the weekends there are street markets or *ferías* (fay-REE-ahs), which sell everything from junk to priceless antiques. Food items such as vegetables and sausages and quick lunches are also sold.

VACATION TIME

During the summer (December to March), most Uruguayans living in or near Montevideo will spend weekends

Secondhand clothing is displayed for sale at a street market in Montevideo.

and holidays at one of the many beaches strung out along the drive from the capital to Punta del Este. Those keeping an eye on expenses will either go for just a day or will look for economical cottages to rent. Those with more money to spend have villas or can afford to rent homes in Punta del Este for the two-month summer vacation. Wherever vacationers end up, however, summertime will be family barbecue time. Every rental house and villa has its own outdoor wood-fired barbecue, and the most popular summer food is grilled meat.

PUNTA DEL ESTE Punta del Este is the main tourist resort in Uruguay. When it is open during the summer, it is the place to be. Located to the east of Montevideo, Punta del Este has a 25-mile (40-km) stretch of beach. Its beauty is comparable to the fabled resort areas of the French Riviera. Throughout the season, there are many sport competitions there and activities for singles and families. It is as if the cultural heartbeat of Uruguay shifts for the summer season from Montevideo to Punta del Este. There are open-air concerts, theatrical performances and premieres, dance performances, and recitals that are held at the two big clubs: Club del Lago and the Cantegril.

Piriapolis is just one of Uruguay's many beach resort towns.

There are also local-level sport competitions and beauty contests. The seashore season ends with the Festival of the Sea. After that, everyone packs up and goes home for another ten months of life in the city.

PIRIAPOLIS Piriapolis, also to the east of Montevideo, was Uruguay's first seaside resort. It was founded in 1893 by Francisco Piria, who built the mellow landmark Argentino Hotel there. Piriapolis is still an active resort town, but it is much quieter than Punta del Este. It attracts people who want a more restful vacation than the wild nights Punta del Este provides. Recently, thermal baths using heated ocean water have opened. People now visit Piriapolis especially for the health and beauty spas.

OTHER DESTINATIONS Uruguayans who prefer something different can venture to the interior of the country for a vacation. Some popular destinations include the thermal springs near Salto and Paysandú in the northwest. The springs there result from warm water bubbling up to the surface, creating inviting pools. Family resorts have been built around the springs, with hotels, movie theaters, shopping areas, and restaurants.

Sea lions sit on a rocky promontory off the isolated hamlet of Cabo Polonio on the Atlantic.

For those interested in nature, there is Rocha department in the southeast. There the coast is much rockier and, being on the Atlantic Ocean, the water is rougher. Small fishing villages are scattered along the coast, and the shore rocks support a large colony of sea lions. Fishing enthusiasts find boats for hire, and nature lovers enjoy the wild feeling of the remote Rocha seacoast.

Inland, there are parks and nature reserves that are home to Uruguay's wildlife. Some of those beautiful parks permit hunting and fishing, while others are for observation only.

Motorists also enjoy taking country drives throughout the year to see the fantastic scenery of the plains. Some of the old ranch houses are open for guests as bed-and-breakfast inns—new life for classic estancias.

INTERNET LINKS

https://www.independent.co.uk/travel/americas/uruguay-football -team-argentina-euros-luis-suarez-a7125561.html
This colorful article describes Uruguay's passion for soccer.

https://www.lonelyplanet.com/uruguay/activities/a/pa-act/363445
This travel site provides ideas for leisure activities in Uruguay.

http://www.viven.com.uy/571/eng/default.asp
This is the official website of the Andes plane crash incident.

FESTIVALS

Colorfully clad participants ride in the Patria Gaucha Festival.

THE SEPARATION OF CHURCH AND state is taken quite seriously in Uruguay. As such, all religious holidays in Uruguay have been secularized. Religious folks are free to worship on those days, but officially, from the state's point of view, the traditional Christian celebrations have different, nonreligious names. For example, Easter Week is called Semana Criolla ("Creole Week," a gaucho festival) or Semana de Turismo, ("Tourism Week"). Christmas is "Family Day."

As in any nation, there are also other patriotic holidays which celebrate important moments in Uruguayan history.

EPIPHANY

In many Roman Catholic countries, Epiphany, January 6, is as important as Christmas. It's the day when the Three Kings, or the Three Wise Men, visited Jesus and presented him with gifts. The Uruguayan secular name for this holiday is Children's Day.

In Uruguay, the holiday has become an African-Uruguayan celebration. Historically, enslaved Africans who had converted to Christianity (as most were compelled to do) celebrated Epiphany as the

12

CALENDAR OF FESTIVALS AND IMPORTANT DAYS

January 1 . . . . New Year's Day (national holiday)

January 6 . . . . Children's Day (Epiphany, Day of Saint Balthazar)

February/March . . . Carnival (Mardi Gras)

March/April . . . . . Semana Criolla, or Tourism Week (Easter Week)

March/April . . . . . Fiesta del Mar, or Festival of the Sea

April 19 . . . . Landing of the Oriental Thirty-three

May 1 . . . . Labor Day (national holiday)

May 18 . . . . Day of the Battle of Las Piedras

June 19 . . . . Birthday of General José Artigas

July 18 . . . . Constitution Day (national holiday)

August 25 . . . . . . Independence Day (national holiday)

October 12 . . . . . Discovery of America

November 2 . . . . . All Souls' Day

December 8 . . . . . Beach Day

December 25 . . . . . Family Day (Christmas) (national holiday)

day when the black king, Balthazar, visited Jesus. As one of the Three Kings, or Wise Men, Balthazar was later made a saint.

Most blacks lived in Montevideo throughout the colonial period and into the nineteenth century. At that time they organized themselves into groups called nations, based on their areas of origin in Africa. Those black nations were mutual-aid societies, meaning that members helped each other in times of need. Each nation also sponsored its own dance and parade group. Periodically through the year, the nations would organize dance celebrations known as candombes. Each nation elected a king and queen for every candombe; then they would compete with other kings and queens to be judged the best dancers.

On Epiphany, African Uruguayans of Montevideo today organize an exceptionally large candombe celebration. The nations parade throughout the city, each playing its own music and dancing in their group's competitions.

CARNIVAL

Carnival is a festival that has been celebrated in Europe since the Middle Ages. It has a long tradition in the New World—particularly in Latin America—and has been celebrated in Montevideo since the earliest colonial times. The name comes from the Latin *carne vale*, which means "farewell to meat."

Similar to Mardi Gras in New Orleans, the festival take place just prior to the Roman Catholic observation of Lent, the forty-day period leading to Easter. During Lent, practicing Catholics give up eating meat or make other sacrifices to prepare for the death of Christ on Good Friday. Carnival is everyone's last chance to feast, eat meat, and celebrate before the solemn time of Lenten sacrifice begins.

In Uruguay, Carnival is a secular, syncretic cultural event that incorporates African and Spanish influences. Unlike some shorter celebrations in other countries, Uruguay's Carnival lasts from mid-January to the end of February. The festivity is marked by parades, music, dancing, drumming, and other performances.

The African-Uruguayan community is famous for the dance groups it sends to the colorful processions. A Queen of Carnival is elected as the most beautiful girl in Montevideo. There are light shows in the streets and an atmosphere of general revelry.

A costumed man takes part in Carnival in Montevideo.

One distinctive feature of the Montevideo Carnival is the street theater or *tablado*. Tablados are makeshift stages where murgas can showcase the performance that they have been practicing for Carnival. Murgas and other carnival groups are invited to perform at various street theaters, or at the Teatro de Verano (summer theater), a big outdoor amphitheater where murga contests are held. Townspeople build huge stages on street corners and hire writers and directors to create plays in which the local people will act. Different communities compete earnestly with one another to put on the best tablado and will spend a lot of money to make their play the most spectacular with lights and set decorations. The plays are usually pure fantasy

FESTIVAL FOR THE GODDESS OF THE SEA

Centuries ago, when African people were shipped to South America as slaves, they brought with them the culture and religion of their homelands, mostly in Western Africa. Much of this heritage was eventually lost in the New World, but remnants live on, and can be found today in music, dance, cuisines, and syncretic beliefs. In the Americas, the African traditions often mixed with European ones to create new versions. In religious beliefs, these adaptations are described as syncretic—a fusion of different or even opposing belief systems.

One particularly important African deity who is still revered today in parts of Africa and South America is the African goddess of the sea. In various parts of Africa, she is known as Yemaya or Yemoja, and in some places, as Mama Watta (Mother Water, or Mother of the Waves). In Uruguay, she is venerated by practitioners of Umbanda, a syncretic Afro-Brazilian religion as Yemanjá (im-an-ZHAH), the patron saint of sailors and fishermen. Sometimes portrayed as a mermaid, she is associated with the spirits of water, the moon, feminine creation, and procreation.

On February 2, Yemanjá Day, celebrations take place on beaches in Montevideo, especially in the Playa Ramirez neighborhood. Offerings of fruits and flowers are piled on altars adorned with blue and white decorations. Many nonbelievers come to enjoy the festivities as well, which include dancing and drumming into the night.

or romance, but sometimes they make fun of local politicians or international celebrities. Musicians also create special songs for the tablados murgas. They often have a political or witty observation in the lyrics.

Although Carnival officially lasts three days, the dancers and theater groups continue to perform in public parks and hotels for a month or more.

SEMANA CRIOLLA

In place of the religious celebrations of Easter, Uruguayans prefer to remember their own cultural past. Semana Criolla, or Creole Week, is named in remembrance of the first descendants of Europeans born in the New World, called creoles, or *criollos* (kree-OHL-yohs) in Spanish. The main motif of the week is to recall and celebrate the gauchos. Men wear typical gaucho clothing and paraphernalia take part in various contests of gaucho skills, including riding bulls, breaking broncos, and trick riding.

Only thirty men are allowed to compete, and they are carefully chosen among applicants from all over the country. Winners take prizes for the best costume, riding equipment, dancing, singing, lassoing, and bronco busting. Women also compete; Uruguayans still remember a woman competitor named Nieves Mira who was very beautiful and talented. Another famous gaucho was El Fantasma, or The Ghost. He was an African Uruguayan who did trick riding with a poncho covering his eyes!

The gaucho events are quite spectacular and many tourists pour into Montevideo to see the competitions. That is why Semana Criolla is also called Tourism Week.

Horsemen demonstrate their skills during Semana Criolla.

FIESTA DEL MAR

The very popular Fiesta del Mar ("Festival of the Sea") takes place at the end of the southern hemisphere's summer, around March or April. (It is not to be confused with the Goddess of the Sea Festival on February 2.) At night the beach between Punta del Este and Punta Ballena is brightly lit with lights. The first part of the celebration is a parade of colorfully decorated boats. Later, a Queen of the Sea is crowned at one of the social clubs on the beach.

Contestants for the coveted royal title wait on the shore for a swimmer dressed as Neptune, the Roman sea god, to emerge from the water. He will approach the winner and place a crown on her head. The Queen will then be paraded through Punta del Este, with a long train of cars following her float. The celebration ends with an hour-long fireworks display, officially ending the summer as well.

HISTORICAL HOLIDAYS

The most important of the national holidays is Independence Day, on August 25, when ceremonies are held in Independence Square in Montevideo.

Constitution Day, on July 18, celebrates the first constitution drafted and signed in 1830. Finally, April 19 is the day when everyone remembers the 1823 landing in Montevideo of the Oriental Thirty-three—a group of revolutionaries led by Juan Antonio Lavalleja—striving to free Uruguay from the Brazilians. All of these historic days are public holidays and occasions to display heartfelt patriotism. As is true of patriotic holidays anywhere, politicians and other important citizens use the occasions to deliver ceremonious speeches.

Two days are devoted to the memory of General José Artigas. One is on June 19, which commemorates his birthday. The other is May 18, which celebrates his famous victory at the Battle of Las Piedras. Las Piedras is a village not far from Montevideo where, in 1811, Artigas and his small band of soldiers confronted Spanish loyalists. After six hours of combat, Artigas emerged victorious.

The battle is not significant because of the number of Spanish losses or the scale of the victory but because its triumph gave people hope that the Spaniards could be beaten. As a result of his victory, Artigas was able to rally a large force of men when he marched out of Montevideo. That event made Artigas famous as "the chief of the Orientals," as Uruguayans were called at the time.

BEACH DAY

Uruguay is south of the equator, so the seasons are reversed. December 8 is the official opening of the beaches and the beginning of the summer vacation period for Uruguayans. Before anyone steps into the ocean, a priest blesses the waters to make them safe. There are also regattas, or sailing races, at various ports. In Carrasco there is an international shooting competition.

CHRISTMAS

Christmas in Uruguay is a very different sort of holiday from what it is in Europe and North America. Taking place at in the summer, it is typically a long, hot day with many hours of sunlight. On Christmas Eve, families will often enjoy a big *asado* (barbecue) meal, set off fireworks after dark, and children will stay up until midnight to receive their gifts. Although religious Christians may attend church services, most families celebrate December 25 as Día de la Familia, and may spend the day at the beach.

Nevertheless, Christmas traditions from Nordic countries have migrated to Uruguay, where they show up incongruously as fake snow on fake pine trees, fur-bedecked Papa Noels (Santas), and the like. December 25 is a national holiday, and most people have the day off. Since children are already on summer break from school, there are no Christmas vacations as in the Northern Hemisphere.

INTERNET LINKS

http://darkroom.baltimoresun.com/2017/02/honoring-the-african-sea-goddess-yemanja-in-uruguay/#1
This slide show presents captioned images of the Yemanja Festival in Montevideo.

http://www.guruguay.com/uruguay-festivals-celebrations-yemanja
http://www.guruguay.com/why-uruguayans-celebrate-tourism-week-not-easter
This site provides two good articles about festivals in Uruguay.

https://www.reuters.com/news/picture/the-gauchos-of-uruguay-idUSRTX5E33D
This site presents a slideshow of a gaucho-style rodeo from the 2018 Semana Criolla.

https://theculturetrip.com/south-america/uruguay/articles/montevideo-carnival-what-to-know-about-the-worlds-longest-party
Plenty of information and colorful photos of Carnival are featured on this site.

FOOD

Fresh vegetables beckon at a street market in Old Town Montevideo.

13

REFLECTING THE DEMOGRAPHICS OF the Uruguayan people, the country's cuisine is very European in nature. Spanish influences, in particular, are prevalent in the diet, but gaucho, Italian, and even German traditions are part of the mix. Unlike in some other South American countries, very little remains of the gastronomic heritage of the land's original inhabitants—except for the love of maté.

Uruguayan cuisine is a fusion of several European influences, especially those of Mediterranean origins. Meat is an essential part of the Uruguayan diet, and the favored method of cooking it is on the barbeque grill. The most popular drink is maté.

TYPICAL FOODS AND BEVERAGES

The central dish in all main meals in Uruguay is meat. In the early days of independence and trade with Britain, the main export was not meat but hides for English leather industries. That was because there was no easy way to ship fresh meat in the years before refrigeration. When gauchos rounded up animals for slaughter, they were left with literally tons of meat once the hides were removed. Meat thus became the heartbeat of the Uruguayan diet. Late in the nineteenth century canning technology was developed, and meat could then be exported to Europe.

Asado, or barbecued meat, is perhaps the most popular meal. Asado refers to both the barbecue tradition and the grilled meat itself. All Uruguayan homes have an outdoor grill for this purpose. They burn

Many different kinds and cuts of meat sizzle on an outside grill at a restaurant in Montevideo.

wood or wood charcoal to cook with rather than gas because it gives the meat a more desirable flavor.

Meat is also processed into other forms. A favorite is *moncilla* (mone-SEE-yah), a blood sausage. Meat may also be used in empanadas (aym-pah-NAH-dahs), sweet or savory pastry turnovers. *Chivitos* (chee-VEE-tohs) are a kind of local fast-food sandwich that usually includes tomato, thinly sliced steak, ham, egg, cheese, and lettuce piled high in a bun. Other fast foods using meat are *olímpicos* (oh-LEEM-pee-kohs), *húngaros* (OON-gah-rohs), and *panchos* (PAHN-chohs), or hot dogs. Olímpicos are essentially club sandwiches. Húngaros and panchos are both sausages served on buns like hot dogs, but húngaros are very spicy. A country favorite is meat stew or *estofado* (ay-stoh-FAH-doh). That gaucho favorite originated on the open plains and is very hearty.

A typical family meal includes meat as the main dish (usually beef or chicken) with potatoes, bread, and a green salad or cooked vegetables. Potatoes are the essential accompaniment to huge slabs of steak. Whereas,

According to Guinness World Records, the biggest alfajor *in the world was made in the city of Minas, Uruguay, in December 2010. Measuring 6 ft 3 in (1.91 m) in diameter, and more than 31 inches (80 cm) in height, the gigantic sandwich cookie weighed in at 1,023 pounds (464 kilograms). The alfajor was created to mark the celebration of Uruguay's first National Alfajor Festival, which in turn celebrated the first alfajores that were made in that part of Uruguay sixty years earlier. In order to cook the two cookie layers, a special oversized clay oven was built. The project involved about thirty bakers and assistants.*

in recent years, health-aware North Americans have been eating less red meat and smaller portions, Uruguayans continue to appreciate one-pound cuts on their plates.

With the large numbers of Italian immigrants arriving in the late nineteenth and early twentieth century, Uruguay's diet was supplemented with other foods. Some of the first businesses opened by Italians were pasta-making factories. They also imported their favorite foods such as Parmesan cheese and prosciutto (dry-cured Italian ham). As those became popular in pasta and pizza dishes, Uruguayans began producing their own. Typical Italian-Uruguayan pizza is made in a wood-burning oven in keeping with the barbecue tradition.

The Spanish heritage can be seen in the way seafood and stews are cooked. Many local dishes feature mussels, shrimps, and cockles as well as freshwater and saltwater fish. Along the seacoast, restaurants offer freshly caught fish and shellfish.

Desserts also have been influenced by Uruguay's European heritage. Pastry was introduced by the Italian immigrants, and most cafés feature delicious examples. The Spanish influence on desserts is seen in the frequent use of *dulce de leche* (DOOL-say day LAY-chay, literally sweetness of milk), a kind of thick, concentrated sweetened milk. Dulce is used as a sauce with fruit or spread on bread and pastry. It is incredibly sweet and rich.

Most Uruguayans today do the bulk of their grocery shopping at a supermarket. Before large supermarkets became common, people bought

Yerba maté is a relative of the European holly tree. Its leaves are harvested and dried. A cup of maté is made by packing a cup—usually a maté gourd—full of the leaves and then adding hot water. The mixture is left to steep. When the water is infused with the flavor of the maté, a tea straw, or bombilla, is dipped into the container full of soaked leaves, and the warm liquid is sipped through it. The bombilla has a spoonlike filter tip on the end that goes into the tea that prevents the leaves from being sipped up the straw. Maté is an acquired taste—it is fairly bitter and has an earthy flavor.

Social relevance is attached to maté drinking. Among indigenous peoples, maté drinking was done in small groups, with the cup passed around for everyone to sip. The first Europeans to adopt this social habit were the gauchos who gathered together in small groups around the campfire in the evenings. Not only do people like to drink it all day but, as often as possible, they gather together to share the drink.

Interestingly, during the military dictatorship, when most forms of public meeting were prohibited, maté gatherings remained one of the few ways people could meet legally and talk with one another. Those wanting to pass along information, or simply to be together in social groups, gathered at local maté snack shops. Since there was nothing noticeably political about the practice, the police and army ignored it.

their food from shops specializing in particular products. If they wanted the freshest vegetables, they went to the greengrocer, for meat they visited their local butcher, for fish the fishmonger, and so on. The reason for shopping that way was that most working-class and middle-class people did not have the space or appliances to store food for a long time. They could not freeze food for later use, so they did their shopping every day or every few days. Those specialized stores, however, are no longer as prominent as they once were.

The drink of choice throughout the day is maté, a tea made with the leaves of the yerba maté, which is native to South America. Europeans learned to drink maté from the indigenous peoples. Maté has quite a bit of caffeine and is used a little like coffee in North American culture. Uruguayans drink so much maté, many of them carry a thermos of hot water and a supply of dried leaves everywhere they go so they can prepare fresh cups of the beverage on the spot.

Uruguay produces its own beer and wine. One particularly Uruguayan drink is *clericó* (klay-ree-KOH), which is a mixture of white wine and fruit juice. Sparkling wine mixed with white wine is called *medio y medio* (MAY-dee-oh ee MAY-dee-oh) or "half and half."

MEALTIMES

The Uruguayan pattern of eating is similar to that found in southern Europe. Breakfast for many Uruguayans is a cup of coffee or maté and a large croissant. Working people usually return home for a long lunch break, often lasting from noon or 1 p.m. to 3 or 4 p.m.

Lunch is the main meal of the day. It usually includes a first course such as a salad or soup, a main course of meat and vegetables, and dessert. Since lunch is the heaviest meal of the day, people often take a nap afterward to help with digestion; they then return to work until 7 or 8 p.m. Later in the evening they will have another, lighter meal. Their supper may not be eaten until 10 or 11 at night, which is not very late since they took a nap at midday. The relaxed cultural tradition of taking naps is, however, becoming a thing of the past as demanding work schedules now do not allow most Uruguayans to lie down for a while in the afternoon.

A gaucho sips his maté during a Semana Criolla festival.

EATING OUT

Eating out is very popular in the cities. Montevideo offers every type of restaurant and price range imaginable, and restaurants are open morning, noon, and night. In the mornings, cafés everywhere serve coffee and light breakfasts for people on their way to work.

At midmorning, many workers take a short break from work and gather in cafeterias for some maté or coffee and a chat with coworkers. These corner snack bars are great for mixing all types of people. It is not unusual for blue-collar workers, secretaries, students, and businesspeople to go to the same snack bar.

People who cannot return home for lunch will eat at a restaurant near their workplace or school. Many restaurants cater to those eating out with something called the fixed, three-course menu of the day—a set meal that does not allow customers to choose what they want. The advantage for the restaurant is that there is no need to stock and prepare many different foods; for the thrifty customer, the fixed-price menu is fairly cheap. People often have a favorite place to eat lunch and go there every day.

Customers enjoy their meals at a barbecue restaurant in the capital city.

For the late evening meal, there are a variety of foods and styles of service in Montevideo and other big cities. From Italian gourmet to pizza parlors, from pubs to fancy French restaurants—the diners can take their pick. The most popular type of restaurant, called a *parrillada* (barbecue, or grill), caters to the Uruguayan passion for grilled meat and uses only wood charcoal.

Another specialty restaurant is the gaucho club. The busy clubs are decorated with pictures and mementos of gaucho life. They specialize in gaucho dishes such as *asado con cuero*—large pieces of beef grilled with the hide left on—and *mazamorra* (mah-zah-MOHR-rah), ground corn with milk. For simpler tastes, there are *cervecerías* (sayr-vay-say-REE-ahs) or beer gardens. Along with beer, they serve chivitos—the extra large steak sandwich—and other snack foods. Many of these sorts of places don't even open until at least 10 p.m. for the late night supper crowd.

Away from the larger cities, there are few fancy restaurants and certainly no foreign food. In rural areas, distances are much greater and budgets much tighter, so country people rarely tend to eat out. The core of their diet is still meat and potatoes. Another rural staple is rice, often used as an inexpensive and nutritious filler in soups and stews. Uruguay is an important exporter of rice. People in the countryside eat less fish, being farther from the coast and its bountiful catches.

INTERNET LINKS

http://www.explore-uruguay.com/about-uruguay-food.html
This travel site includes an introduction to Uruguayan cuisine with links to many recipes.

https://theculturetrip.com/south-america/uruguay/articles/a-food -lovers-guide-to-uruguay
The most popular foods of Uruguay are presented, with numerous photos.

CHIVITO

The name of Uruguay's iconic sandwich means "little goat" but there's no goat involved!

2 slices bacon

1 3- or 4-ounce (84—113 grams) beef steak, about ½-inch (1.25 cm) thick (rib-eye, tenderloin, or other tender cut), pounded very thin

Salt, black pepper (to taste)

1 teaspoon butter

1 egg

1 large sandwich bun (such as a ciabatta roll)

1 tablespoon ketchup

1 Tbsp mayonnaise

1 slice each deli ham, tomato, and Monterey Jack cheese

Handful of lettuce leaves

Optional toppings: sliced onions, pickles, roasted sweet peppers

In a large skillet over medium heat, cook the bacon slices until they are crispy. Set aside on paper towels to cool.

Sprinkle steak with salt and black pepper. Pound it out with a mallet until thin. Cook the steak in the skillet over medium hot heat. Cook for about 2 minutes per side, or until it reaches the desired doneness. Set aside.

Wipe the skillet clean. Melt the butter over medium heat and fry the egg sunny-side up until done to preference.

Preheat the broiler.

Spread the inside of both sides of the bun with ketchup and mayonnaise.

Top the bottom half with, a slice of beef, 2 slices of bacon, a slice of ham, a slice of tomato, and a slice of cheese.

Place the uncovered sandwich under the broiler briefly to melt the cheese. Make sure it doesn't burn.

Remove the sandwich from the oven, place the fried egg over the cheese, add the optional topping(s) and lettuce, and then top with the other half of the bun. Serve immediately.

ALFAJORES

Uruguayans love dulce de leche, which is sandwiched here between two shortcake wafers.

1 cup (120 g) cornstarch
¾ cup (90 g) all-purpose flour, plus
   more as needed
1 tsp baking powder
½ tsp baking soda
¼ tsp fine salt
8 Tbsp (120 g) unsalted butter (1 stick),
   room temperature

⅓ cup (35 g) granulated sugar
2 large egg yolks
1 Tbsp brandy; ½ tsp vanilla extract
1 cup (240 milliliters) dulce de leche
   (homemade or store-bought)
Powdered sugar, for dusting

Place the cornstarch, flour, baking powder, baking soda, and salt in a medium bowl and whisk briefly to combine; set aside.

Place the butter and sugar in the bowl of a stand mixer fitted with a paddle attachment. Mix on medium speed until the mixture is light and fluffy, about 3 minutes. Add the egg yolks, brandy, and vanilla and mix until incorporated, about 30 seconds. On low speed, gradually add the reserved flour mixture and mix until just incorporated, about 30 seconds.

Shape dough into a smooth disk and wrap in plastic wrap. Refrigerate at least one hour.

Meanwhile, heat the oven to 350°F (175°C). Line two baking sheets with parchment paper .

Place the unwrapped dough on a lightly floured work surface. Lightly flour the top of the dough. Roll to ¼-inch (0.6 cm) thickness. Stamp out 24 rounds using a 2-inch (5 cm) round cutter, rerolling the dough as necessary until it is all used up.

Place the cookies on the baking sheets, 12 per sheet and at least ½ inch (1.25 cm) apart. Bake 1 sheet at a time until the cookies are firm and pale golden on the bottom, about 12 to 14 minutes. (The cookies will be pale on top.) Transfer to a wire rack to cool completely.

Gently spread about 2 tsps of the dulce de leche on the bottom of half the cookies. Place a second cookie on top and gently press to create a sandwich. Dust with powdered sugar before serving.

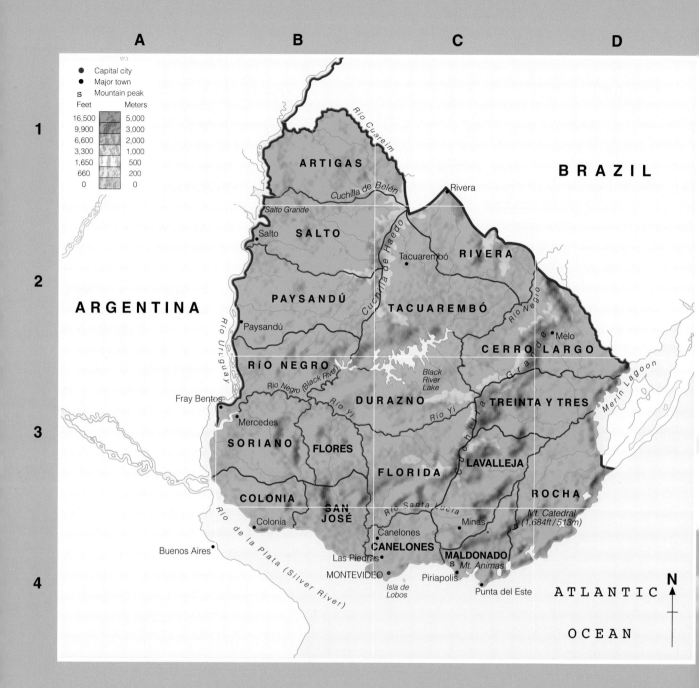

A
B
C
D

1

2

3

4

- Capital city
- Major town
s Mountain peak

Feet | Meters
16,500 | 5,000
9,900 | 3,000
6,600 | 2,000
3,300 | 1,000
1,650 | 500
660 | 200
0 | 0

Río Cuareim

BRAZIL

ARTIGAS

Cuchilla de Belén

Rivera

Salto Grande

Salto

SALTO

RIVERA

Tacuarembó

ARGENTINA

PAYSANDÚ

Cuchilla de Haedo

TACUAREMBÓ

Río Negro

CERRO LARGO

Melo

Paysandú

Río Uruguay

RÍO NEGRO

Río Negro (Black River)

Fray Bentos

Mercedes

Río Yi

DURAZNO

Black
River
Lake

Río Yi

Cuchilla Grande

TREINTA Y TRES

Merín Lagoon

SORIANO

FLORES

LAVALLEJA

Cuchilla Grande

ROCHA

COLONIA

FLORIDA

Río Santa Lucia

Mt. Catedral
s (1,684ft / 513m)

Colonia

SAN
JOSÉ

Minas

Buenos Aires

Río de la Plata (Silver River)

Canelones

CANELONES

Las Piedras

MALDONADO

MONTEVIDEO

s Mt. Animas

Piriapolis

*Isla de
Lobos*

Punta del Este

ATLANTIC

OCEAN

N

MAP OF URUGUAY

Argentina, A1—A4, B1—B4
Artigas, B1, C1
Atlantic Ocean, C4, D2, D4

Black River Lake, B3, C2—C3
Brazil, B1, C1—C2, D1—D3
Buenos Aires, A4

Canelones (city), C4
Canelones (province), B4, C4
Cerro Largo, C2—C3, D2—D3
Colonia (city), B4
Colonia (province), B3—B4
Cuchilla de Belén, B1, C1
Cuchilla de Haeddo, B2, C2
Cuchilla Grande, C2—C3, D2

Durazno, B3, C3

Flores, B3
Florida, B3, C3—C4
Fray Bentos, B3

Isla de Lobos, C4

Lavalleja, C3
Las Piedras, C4

Maldonado, C4
Melo, D2
Mercedes, B3
Merín Lagoon, D2—D3
Minas, C4
Montevideo, C4
Mt. Animas, C4
Mt. Catedral, C4

Paysandú (city), B2

Paysandú (province), B2
Piriapolis, C4
Punta del Este, C4

Río Cuareim, B1, C1
Río de la Plata (Silver River), B4
Río de Uruguay, B2—B3
Río Negro (province), B2—B3
Río Negro (Black River), B3, C2, D2
Río Santa Lucia, C4
Río Yi, B3, C3
Rivera (city), C1
Rivera (province), C1—C2
Rocha, C3—C4, D3—D4

Salto (city), B2
Salto (province), B2, C2
Salto Grande, B2
San José, B3—B4
Soriano, B3

Tacuarembó (city), C2
Tacuarembó (province), B2, C2
Treinta Y Tres, C3, D3

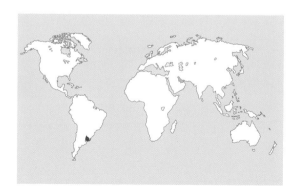

ECONOMIC URUGUAY

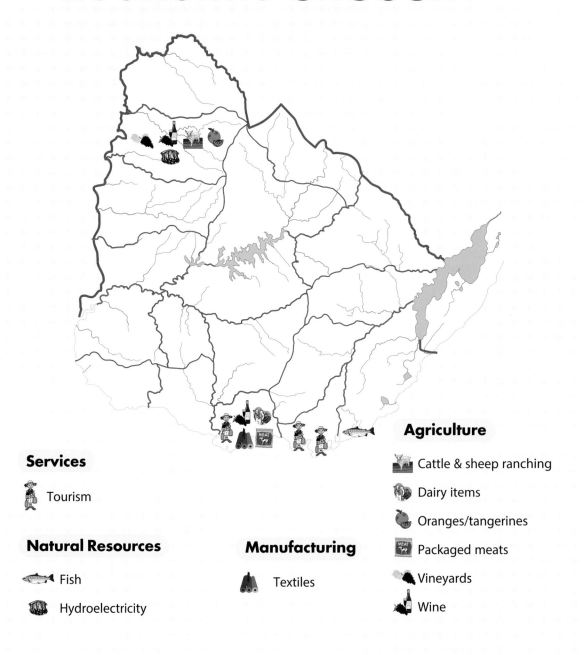

Services

🧍 Tourism

Natural Resources

🐟 Fish

🔋 Hydroelectricity

Manufacturing

🧵 Textiles

Agriculture

🐄 Cattle & sheep ranching

🐑 Dairy items

🍊 Oranges/tangerines

🥩 Packaged meats

🍇 Vineyards

🍷 Wine

ABOUT THE ECONOMY

TYPE OF ECONOMY
Free market

GROSS DOMESTIC PRODUCT (GDP)
Official exchange rate
$60.27 billion (2017)

GDP GROWTH
3.5 percent (2017)

GDP BY SECTOR OF ORIGIN
agriculture: 6.2 percent
industry: 25 percent
services: 68.8 percent (2017)

INFLATION RATE
6.1 percent (2017)

CURRENCY
Uruguay peso (UYU peso)
1 US dollar = 28.30 UYU pesos (2018)

NATURAL RESOURCES
Arable land, pastures, hydroelectric power,
granite, marble, and fisheries

AGRICULTURAL PRODUCTS
Cellulose, beef, soybeans, rice, wheat; dairy
products; fish; lumber, tobacco, wine

INDUSTRY
food processing, electrical machinery,
transportation equipment, petroleum
products, textiles, chemicals, beverages

MAJOR EXPORTS
beef, soybeans, cellulose, rice, wheat,
wood, dairy products, wool

MAJOR IMPORTS
refined oil, crude oil, passenger and other
transportation vehicles, vehicle parts,
cellular phones

EXPORT PARTNERS
Brazil 16.4 percent, China 12.2 percent, US
6.2 percent, Argentina 5 percent (2016)

IMPORT PARTNERS
China 18.8 percent, Brazil 17.9 percent,
Argentina 13.3 percent, US 6.9 percent,
Germany 4.7 percent (2016)

POPULATION BELOW POVERTY LINE
9.7 percent (2015)

LABOR FORCE
1.748 million (2017)

LABOR FORCE BY OCCUPATION
agriculture: 13 percent
industry: 14 percent
services: 73 percent (2010)

UNEMPLOYMENT RATE
7.3 percent (2017)

CULTURAL URUGUAY

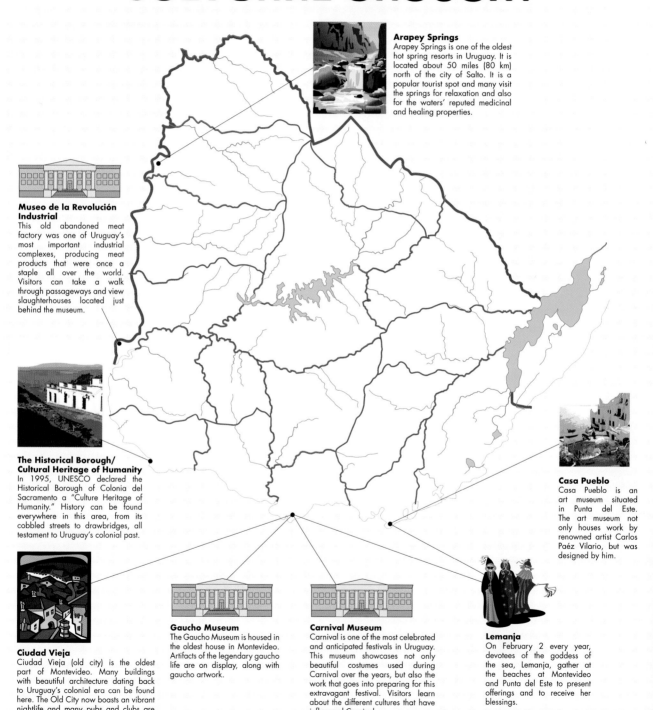

Arapey Springs
Arapey Springs is one of the oldest hot spring resorts in Uruguay. It is located about 50 miles (80 km) north of the city of Salto. It is a popular tourist spot and many visit the springs for relaxation and also for the waters' reputed medicinal and healing properties.

Museo de la Revolución Industrial
This old abandoned meat factory was one of Uruguay's most important industrial complexes, producing meat products that were once a staple all over the world. Visitors can take a walk through passageways and view slaughterhouses located just behind the museum.

The Historical Borough/Cultural Heritage of Humanity
In 1995, UNESCO declared the Historical Borough of Colonia del Sacramento a "Culture Heritage of Humanity." History can be found everywhere in this area, from its cobbled streets to drawbridges, all testament to Uruguay's colonial past.

Casa Pueblo
Casa Pueblo is an art museum situated in Punta del Este. The art museum not only houses work by renowned artist Carlos Paéz Vilario, but was designed by him.

Ciudad Vieja
Ciudad Vieja (old city) is the oldest part of Montevideo. Many buildings with beautiful architecture dating back to Uruguay's colonial era can be found here. The Old City now boasts an vibrant nightlife and many pubs and clubs are found in this district.

Gaucho Museum
The Gaucho Museum is housed in the oldest house in Montevideo. Artifacts of the legendary gaucho life are on display, along with gaucho artwork.

Carnival Museum
Carnival is one of the most celebrated and anticipated festivals in Uruguay. This museum showcases not only beautiful costumes used during Carnival over the years, but also the work that goes into preparing for this extravagant festival. Visitors learn about the different cultures that have influenced Carnival.

Lemanja
On February 2 every year, devotees of the goddess of the sea, Lemanja, gather at the beaches at Montevideo and Punta del Este to present offerings and to receive her blessings.

ABOUT THE CULTURE

OFFICIAL NAME
Oriental Republic of Uruguay

FLAG DESCRIPTION
The flag of Uruguay has a field of nine equal horizontal stripes of white alternating with blue. The stripes represent the nine original counties. A yellow sun, depicting a human face known as the Sun of May, is located in a white square in the upper hoist-side corner. Sixteen sun rays, alternating between triangular and wavy, burst forth from the sun.

POPULATION
3,466,062 (March 2018)

CAPITAL
Montevideo

URBANIZATION
urban population: 95.6 percent of total population (2017)

ETHNIC GROUPS
white 88 percent, mestizo 8 percent, black 4 percent, Amerindian (practically nonexistent)

RELIGIONS
Roman Catholic 47.1 percent; Protestant 11.1 percent; nonaffiliated 23.2 percent; Jewish 0.3 percent; atheist or agnostic 17.2 percent, other 1.1 percent (2006)

MAIN LANGUAGES
Spanish (official), Portuñol, also called Fronterizo or Bayano, Brazilero (Portuguese-Spanish mix on the Uruayan-Brazilian frontier)

INFANT MORTALITY RATE
8.3 deaths / 1,000 live births (2017)

LIFE EXPECTANCY AT BIRTH
77.4 years
male: 74.2 years
female: 80.6 years (2017)

LITERACY RATE
98.5 percent

TIMELINE

IN URUGUAY	IN THE WORLD
	1206 Genghis Khan unifies the Mongols and begins conquest of the world.
	1558–1603 Reign of Elizabeth I of England
1680 Portuguese found Colonia del Sacramento (Uruguay).	
1726 Montevideo is founded.	
1750 The first African slaves arrive in Montevideo.	**1776** US Declaration of Independence
	1789–1799 The French Revolution
1799 José Gervasio Artigas is appointed head of Montevideo militia.	
1811 General José G. Artigas launches a successful revolt against Spain; the Exodus of the Orientals.	
1825 Uruguay declares its independence from Brazil and adheres to a regional federation with Argentina.	
1828 Uruguay becomes an independent state.	
1830 Uruguay's first constitution is adopted. General José Frutuoso Riveria becomes president.	**1861–1865** US Civil War
1865–1870 War of the Triple Alliance (Argentina, Brazil, and Uruguay aligned against Paraguay)	
1903–1907 José Batlle y Ordóñez is elected president.	
1911–1915 José Batlle y Ordóñez is reelected president and initiates Batllismo reforms.	**1914–1919** World War I

IN URUGUAY		IN THE WORLD
	1930	
The first soccer World Cup is held in Montevideo. Uruguay wins.		**1939** World War II
		1949 The North Atlantic Treaty Organization (NATO) is formed.
		1969 Neil Armstrong becomes the first person to walk on the moon.
Repressive dictatorship takes power.	**1973**	**1986** Nuclear power disaster at Chernobyl in Ukraine
Uruguay co-founds MERCOSUR.	**1991**	**1991** Breakup of the Soviet Union
Financial crisis impels up to 15 percent of Uruguay's population to leave the country in search of work.	**2001**	**2001** Terrorists attack the US on 9/11.
Tabaré Vázquez wins the presidency.	**2004**	**2003** War in Iraq begins.
Uruguay pays off its billion-dollar debt to the International Monetary Fund.	**2006**	**2008** US elects first African American president, Barack Obama.
Jose Mujica is elected president.	**2010**	
Amnesty law that protected officers accused of crimes during military rule is revoked.	**2011**	
Uruguay legalizes marijuana.	**2013**	
Tabaré Vázquez is again elected president.	**2014**	**2015** ISIS launches terror attacks in Europe.
General Gregorio Alvarez, last Uruguayan dictator, dies in prison.	**2016**	**2017** Donald Trump becomes US president. Hurricanes devastate Houston, Caribbean islands, and Puerto Rico.
Uruguay experiences worst drought in a decade.	**2018**	**2018** Winter Olympics in South Korea

GLOSSARY

Batllismo (bahj-JEES-moh)
Government and social reform designed by José Batlle at the beginning of the twentieth century.

bombilla (bohm-BEE-ya)
Straw, usually silver, used to sip maté.

candombe (can-DOHM-bay)
Music and dance of African-Uruguayan origin.

Cocoliche (ko-ko-LEE-chay)
A Spanish-Italian dialect spoken by first-generation Italian immigrants in Buenos Aires and Montevideo.

criollos (kree-OHL-yohs)
Creoles, the first people of European descent born in the New World.

estancia
Large ranch.

Fronterizo (fron-tayr-EE-zoh)
Dialect (also called Portuñol and Bayano) that is a mix of Spanish and Portuguese spoken on the Brazilian-Uruguayan border.

garra charrúa (GAR-rah char-ROO-ah)
(charrúan talon) Expression meaning brave, persistent, and fierce.

gaucho
Traditional cowboy of the southern regions of South America.

Lunfardo (loon-FAR-doh)
Working-class slang used in Buenos Aires and Montevideo.

maté
Herbal steeped beverage made with dried yerba maté leaves.

MERCOSUR (Southern Cone Common Market)
The 1991 free trade agreement between Uruguay, Paraguay, Brazil, and Argentina.

mestizo
Person of mixed Spanish and Indian blood.

murga (MOOR-gah)
Carnival music group and their songs.

Porteño (por-TAYN-yoh)
A variety of Spanish spoken in Buenos Aires and Montevideo.

rastra (RAHS-trah)
Wide belt made of leather and metal worn by gauchos.

tablado (tah-BLAH-doh)
Neighborhood street theater performed during Carnival.

Tupamaros (too-pah-MAR-ohs)
Guerrilla fighters who challenged the government before the military dictatorship.

yerba maté
Plant whose dried leaves are used to steep the Uruguayan tealike drink called maté.

FOR FURTHER INFORMATION

BOOKS

Burford, Tim. *Uruguay* (Bradt Travel Guide) Chalfont St Peter: England, 2018.

ONLINE

BBC News. http://news.bbc.co.uk/2/hi/americas/country_profiles/1229360.stm

CIA World Factbook. https://www.cia.gov/library/publications/the-world-factbook /geos/uy.html

Encyclopaedia Britannica. https://www.britannica.com/place/Uruguay

Lonely Planet. https://www.lonelyplanet.com/uruguay

The Culture Trip. Uruguay. https://theculturetrip.com/south-america/uruguay

MUSIC CD

Jaime Roos. *Candombe, Murga y Rocanrol*. Sony Music, 2004.

Los Olimarenos. *Mis 30 Mejores Canciones*. Sony BMG Europe, 2007.

FILM

El Baño del Papa. Directed by César Charlone and Enrique Fernández. Film Movement, 2007.

BIBLIOGRAPHY

Albarenga, Pablo. "Where Did Uruguay's Indigenous Population Go?" *El País*, November 10, 2017. https://elpais.com/elpais/2017/11/06/inenglish/1509969553_044435.html.

BBC News. "Uruguay Country Profile." http://news.bbc.co.uk/2/hi/americas/country_profiles/1229360.stm.

———."Uruguay Timeline." http://news.bbc.co.uk/2/hi/americas/country_profiles/1229362.stm.

CIA World Factbook. "Uruguay." https://www.cia.gov/library/publications/the-world-factbook/geos/uy.html.

Fajardo, Milena. "Montevideo Carnival: What to Know About the World's Longest Party." *The Culture Trip*, November 14, 2017. https://theculturetrip.com/south-america/uruguay/articles/montevideo-carnival-what-to-know-about-the-worlds-longest-party.

Oya, Solansh. "Maintaining Excellent Water Quality in Uruguay," *Borgen Magazine*, May 31, 2017. http://www.borgenmagazine.com/maintaining-water-quality-in-uruguay.

Overseas Security Advisory Council (OSAC). "Uruguay 2017 Crime and Safety Report." US Department of State Bureau of Diplomatic Security. April 10, 2017. https://www.osac.gov/pages/ContentReportDetails.aspx?cid=21623.

Parks, Ken. "Uruguay Spends $2.6 Billion to Become South America Wind Leader." *Renewable Energy World*, June 17, 2015. http://www.renewableenergyworld.com/news/2015/06/uruguay-spends-26-billion-to-become-south-america-wind-leader.html.

Romero, Simon and Mauricio Rabuffetti. "Tabaré Vázquez Reclaims Presidency in Uruguay Election." *The New York Times*. November 30, 2014. https://www.nytimes.com/2014/12/01/world/americas/leftist-tabar-vzquez-reclaims-presidency-in-uruguay-election.html.

INDEX

143

INDEX